ENDORSEMENTS

"One of the passions of my heart is to see people receive all that Jesus paid for on the cross. So many believers stop short of receiving the fullness that is available to them through the work of Christ's sacrifice. It is time for the lies that are robbing people from their inheritance in the Kingdom to be broken so they can walk in the freedom made possible through Jesus. The work that has been pioneered through the ministry of Sozo for decades has seen incredible fruit and impact in this area of freedom. The revelation Sozo ministers walk in and the tools they use have brought freedom and joy to countless lives. My prayer is that this book will continue to bring people into a place of fullness and freedom that is available for all who will receive it."

BANNING LIEBSCHER
Founder and Pastor of Jesus Culture,
Author of *Rooted, Jesus Culture: Calling a Generation to Revival* and *Journey of a World Changer: 40 Days to Ignite a Life that Transforms the World*

"It is with great joy I recommend to you Dawna De Silva and Teresa Liebscher's book *Sozo: Saved, Healed, Delivered*. They have championed this message so profoundly that people all over the world are living in a freedom they never thought was possible. In reading this book, you will find insight, inspiration, and practical tools to assist in the lifestyle Jesus always intended. Read it and be changed!"

BILL JOHNSON
Senior Leader, Bethel Church, Redding, California
Author of *When Heaven Invades Earth*

"Over the years, I've had the honor of watching Dawna and Teresa use the Sozo method to help bring hundreds of people into freedom. *Sozo: Saved, Healed, Delivered* is packed full of tools that will help people reach their full potential in their spiritual life. I believe that because of this book, doors will be opened into people's lives, and they will learn to live a life of freedom. Both Dawna and Teresa have a heart for serving and helping people walk in complete freedom. I have no doubt this book will be liberating for those who read it. Thank you, Dawna and Teresa, for writing this book."

BENI JOHNSON
Pastor of Bethel Church, Redding, California
Author of *The Happy Intercessor* and *Healthy and Free*

"Dawna De Silva and Teresa Liebscher's new book, *Sozo: Saved, Healed, Delivered,* is a welcome addition to the area of inner healing, deliverance, and physical healing. There are many insights in the book that can help the ministering person see a breakthrough in his or her ministry. Their ministry is impacting leaders and churches around the world. I recently met key leaders in Nigeria that are going through the Sozo training to bring this training to Nigeria. Perhaps you should read the book, receive the training, and bring it to your local church."

RANDY CLARK, D.MIN.
Author of *There is More, Power to Heal,* and
Co-author of *Essential Guide to Healing*

"Dawna De Silva and Teresa Liebscher have decades of combined experience in navigating the spirit realm and setting people free. Literally thousands of people have been released from chains of darkness into their calling in Christ through their ministry! Dawna and Teresa's new book, *Sozo: Saved, Healed, Delivered,* will first and foremost lead you into a relationship with the Author of Freedom, and will illuminate the way to an abundant and whole life. You won't want to miss this book!"

KRIS VALLOTTON
Senior Associate Leader, Bethel Church, Redding, CA
Co-Founder of Bethel School of Supernatural Ministry
Author of eleven books, including
The Supernatural Ways of Royalty and *Spirit Wars.*

"I am so proud of Dawna and Teresa—how they have searched the Scriptures and inquired of the Holy Spirit; how they obey like champions in the face of a challenge, yet remain quiet and devoted to Christ in their daily lives. These are the founders and co-leaders of Bethel's Sozo Ministry. I am as convinced as anyone can be that Dawna and Teresa have mastered a weapon of the Spirit. Our enemy hopes to orphan people, where Bethel Sozo steps in to untangle those plans. This ministry has operated quietly and powerfully for nearly two decades. Over that time, thousands of people have experienced remarkable breakthrough and divine encounters in the areas of their struggle. I am one of those beneficiaries, and you can be, too. Dawna and Teresa have gathered together inspired lessons and secrets for us to learn and apply. Presenting them in a simple and clear model is their gift to you. God bless you as you read this book. I pray you will overcome every struggle, as is every believer's portion in Christ. God bless your prosperous soul."

STEPHEN DE SILVA
CFO of Bethel Church, Redding, California, and
Founder of Prosperous Soul Ministries
Author of *Money and the Prosperous Soul*

"It has been my pleasure to be in ministry for over 30 years now. I have experienced great breakthroughs in my own life and the lives of those I have ministered to, often by removing the blockages or places of unbelief in our hearts. We have all been hurt in life in some way or another and often carry these wounds, offenses, and negative expectations forward—even with God.

"Many of my friends, family, and, of course, I myself have all gone through the Sozo Ministry with amazing results! Sozo contains wonderful keys to receiving the fullness of the freedom Jesus paid for!

"It would be my recommendation that as you read this book, you would keep your heart open to the Holy Spirit as He leads you into more and more freedom—for yourself, and also for all those you come across in everyday life."

CAROL ARNOTT
Co-Leader, Catch The Fire Ministries

"There is nothing more precious than a counselor who will take people by the hand and lead them into a living encounter with the Lord Jesus Christ. Finding such counselors is a monumental task, for they are one in a million. Dawna and Teresa are such counselors. Their new book, *Sozo: Saved, Healed, Delivered,* is full of stories of Sozo sessions in which hurting people are brought into the presence of the Wonderful Counselor where they see, hear and feel His wisdom and comfort.

Thank you, Dawna and Teresa, for the gift of yourselves to the Body of Christ. May you raise up thousands of additional counselors to work alongside you in the Sozo Ministry who are also able to do what you have modeled so beautifully."

DR. MARK VIRKLER
Best-selling author of *4 Keys to Hearing God's Voice*

"Traveling the world the way that my husband Jack Frost and I have done over the last 25 years, you tend to pick up other people's emotional baggage along the way. Add that to your own stuff and all of a sudden you become stuck in situational circumstances and have no clue how you got stuck in life.

"Because the term "Inner Healing" and "Sozo" have been given a bad rap at times, it might cause you to become afraid to try and get healing from outside sources. My question is *why?* People lie to themselves to comfort their walk in the flesh. My husband, Jack, and I always went to outside sources each year for the Father to speak to us so we could deal with any behaviors that might hinder us from being carriers of God's love to our families first, then to the world.

"Even after my husband was diagnosed with cancer we headed out to Redding to go through the Sozo ministry there. In the midst of our greatest battle in life we found hope that motivated us to continue our race because we chose to go through the Sozo Ministry at Bethel that is headed up by these two wonderful ladies.

"Not everyone can go to Redding so I am so excited that *Sozo: Saved, Healed, Delivered* has been penned from the experiences of these two experts: Dawna De Silva and Teresa Liebscher. Jack finished his race well and I have found the courage to move forward because of this wonderful ministry."

TRISHA FROST
Co-Founder Shiloh Place Ministries
Author, *Unbound: Breaking Free of Life's Entanglements*

"As a medical doctor, when I first saw Sozo being demonstrated by Dawna De Silva I thought to myself, *'That is like a very fine set of surgical tools being used by a very skilled surgeon to take away something harmful to health.'*

"That was in 2008, and since that time, my appreciation of Dawna De Silva, Teresa Liebscher, and Sozo has grown. We have established Sozo as a very valuable tool at Eastgate, and hundreds of people have benefitted, finding increased freedom, peace, joy, and physical and spiritual well-being as God works to demonstrate His love.

"As with any other sharp tool, Sozo needs to be used by trained and experienced people in order to get the best outcome. In this book, Dawna and Teresa helpfully instruct us and demonstrate how Sozo works and how we can use the tool kit effectively.

"In the context of health and well-being from a holistic perspective, my experience has shown me that Sozo is a very valuable tool to have available and also that it sits very well alongside other tools such as counseling and medical intervention. I recommend this book to you."

DR. PETE CARTER, MBChB
Medical General Practitioner and
Director of Eastgate, United Kingdom
Author of *Unwrapping Lazarus*
www.eastgate.org.uk

"It is such a privilege to be part of God's healing army in today's world. Father God is working overtime to bring healing to the Bride as He prepares her for His Son. He has raised up many servants such as Dawna and Teresa to be His instruments of healing. Sozo is quick to learn, easy to apply, and effective in results. The deep insights illustrated in this book will accelerate your abilities, enabling you to be fruitful as you join in His healing movement. Thank you, Dawna and Teresa, for adding to the revelation of how to receive God's healing."

CHESTER AND BETSY KYLSTRA
Founders of Restoring The Foundations Ministries
Authors of *Restoring The Foundations,*
An Integrated Approach to Biblical Healing Ministry,
RTF Issue-Focused Ministry, Shame-Fear-Control Stronghold, and more.

Dawna De Silva and Teresa Liebscher's new book, *Sozo,* is a guidebook to finding freedom and wholeness by relating to the Father, Jesus, and Holy Spirit. They have done a masterful job of clearly communicating in a simple and understandable way, how to connect to the Godhead and overcome strongholds that keep us from fulfilling our destinies. The foundational revelation in this book will open the door to the abundant life in Christ that God intended for you. I highly recommend it!

JASON VALLOTTON
Pastoral Care Overseer, Bethel Church, Redding, CA
Author of *The Supernatural Power of Forgiveness*
and *Outrageous Courage.*

SOZO

SAVED | HEALED | DELIVERED

SOZO

SAVED | HEALED | DELIVERED

*A Journey into Freedom
with the Father, Son,
and Holy Spirit*

DAWNA DE SILVA | TERESA LIEBSCHER

DESTINY IMAGE® PUBLISHERS, INC.

P.O. Box 310, Shippensburg, PA 17257-0310

"Promoting Inspired Lives."

This book and all other Destiny Image and Destiny Image Fiction books are available at Christian bookstores and distributors worldwide.

Cover design by Bethel Media

Interior design by Terry Clifton

For more information on foreign distributors, call 717-532-3040.

Reach us on the Internet: www.destinyimage.com.

ISBN 13 TP: 978-0-7684-0915-4

ISBN 13 eBook: 978-0-7684-0916-1

For Worldwide Distribution, Printed in the U.S.A.

1 2 3 4 5 6 7 8 / 20 19 18 17 16

DEDICATIONS

Teresa:

This book is dedicated to my amazing family: Larry, Brandy, Banning, SeaJay, Elli, Raya, and Lake. My life is forever full with you all in it.

Dawna:

I dedicate this book to my champion of 35 years, Stephen De Silva; our mighty men, Cory and Tim; and their wives, Colleen and Autumn.

Bethel Sozo:

We would like to dedicate this book to our ever-increasing Sozo family around the world who, tirelessly and with great joy continue to set the captives free.

ACKNOWLEDGEMENTS

We gratefully give thanks to:

Bill Johnson for modeling how to host God's presence.

Beni Johnson for covering the Sozo Ministry in its infancy and releasing its mantle to us.

Kris Vallotton for his prophetic oversight, teachings on deliverance, and impartation to us.

Danny Silk for championing us and encouraging us to take our ministry to the nations.

Stephen De Silva for his faithful love and support for Dawna and the Sozo Ministry.

Cory De Silva for all the hours spent dreaming, planning, writing, and rewriting this manuscript.

Susan Anderson, Pam Spinosi, and Darryl Cocup for contributing valuable ideas, editing, and content.

Fred Grewe, Pablo Bottari, Alan Ray, Ed Smith, and Aiko Horman for their teachings that catapulted us into creating an international deliverance and inner healing ministry.

Previous generals of inner healing and deliverance ministries for paving the way for this "newbie" Sozo Ministry to flourish.

The regional directors and Sozo teams worldwide who have watched Father God, Jesus, and Holy Spirit connect globally with His sons and daughters.

AUTHORS' NOTE

The stories in this Sozo book, while faithfully representing each account of a person's freedom, have been modified to protect the person's identity. Otherwise, they represent real people in authentic situations.

CONTENTS

FOREWORD

My wife, Sheri, and I struggled for years to overcome generations of dysfunctional family and relationship practices. Our conversion to Christianity, although transformational, left places of unsuccessful paradigms and interactions between us, even though we were committed to preserving our marriage. Years dragged on and our unhealthy practices continued. The distance between us grew. Later, having three children added to our stress. On top of that, we decided to pastor a church. The impending explosion seemed like it would destroy more than just our marriage.

In our second year as pastors, we were introduced to Sozo. We were told it was a "gentler" form of deliverance. We had been through enough deliverance ministries to recognize that such processes could be scary. As scared as we were, we knew we needed help. Sozo could just be our ticket to success in marriage. Fortunately, Sheri went first.

Sheri returned home late from her Sozo session. I was excited to hear what had happened. Since her family had not been a safe environment to grow up in, she, no doubt, had plenty of issues to work through. For years, I prayed for a miracle to change our relationship from fear to peace and joy.

"How was it?" I asked.

"Good," Sheri said. "It was much better than I expected. I heard Father God clearly. He showed me an issue I've been dealing with for a long time but never understood."

At Sheri's response, my heart leaped. My prayers were being answered! Through the Lord's grace, Sheri had received a revelation.

Now she could renounce ties with her history of abuse—all the things that were ruining our marriage. This was the moment I had been waiting for.

Sheri went on to say, "Father God showed me that I've never felt protected."

Nearly leaping from my seat, I thought, "Exactly! You grew up in such a scary place—how could you ever feel protected!" I could not wait to hear the rest of her story.

With a gentle voice, Sheri continued, "God showed me how I've never felt protected…by *you* in our marriage."

Sheri's words deflated my pride. First, I experienced shock, then disbelief. "You mean you never felt protected in your family?"

"Of course I've never felt protected in my family, but I didn't really expect to be safe in that environment. I did, though, expect to feel safe in my marriage to a godly man."

Cue the supernatural brick of revelation. Somehow, Sheri received a Sozo and I experienced deliverance. After twelve years of disconnection, Sheri and I were handed a key. By the end of that year, our marriage changed. Breaking through the denial that I somehow contributed to the breakdown in our marriage, I realized something important. In all my dealings with Sheri's rage, I had never seen it as fear. I always rolled it into her "issues bag" and accused her of being selfish. I would then exercise my own type of selfishness by abandoning her.

The Father's revelation opened my eyes to see Sheri's need for protection. My instinct in prior years had been to protect everyone but Sheri. I figured, because of her aggressiveness, she could take care of herself. As I saw who she truly was, my behavior of respect, support, and protection replaced my natural destructive patterns. Enlightened, I could not believe that I had never thought to protect my wife. After that experience, Sheri abandoned anger as her primary source of communication.

I am sure much of this breakthrough in our marriage had to do with the adjustments I made to bring connection rather than separation. Today, tens of thousands of people benefit from the healing of our marriage. For over a decade, we have shared our story in books, conferences, and trainings around the world. A huge key to our success was this simple, powerful experience that created an avalanche of new opportunities for the Silks.

The Gospel of Jesus Christ is not limited to salvation from hell. It intends to lead us all to freedom, power, and love for our lives here on earth. The tools you will learn in this book are a gift from God. They will establish connections with the Godhead, help you to remove lies hindering your life, and empower you to see things through God's perspective. If this is your first time reading this material, be patient. Understand that Sozo's aim is to increase your ability to hear God's voice and to introduce you to the truth about who He is, who you are, and how you can live victoriously in your life, family, and destiny.

Dawna and Teresa are proven authorities who release people into freedom. They are leaders of a global movement who train Christians to apply tools to their lives in dozens of countries and cultures around the world.

Spiritual authority comes through aligning the truth of Heaven against the lies of this world. Powerful adjustments, abundance, and freedom come from this simple yet effective process. I have no doubt you will benefit greatly from these following pages.

Blessings,
DANNY SILK
President, Loving On Purpose
Author, *Keep Your Love On, Culture of Honor,*
Loving Our Kids on Purpose
Currently serving on the
Senior Leadership Teams of Bethel Church,
Redding, and Jesus Culture, Sacramento

INTRODUCTION

Building a strong connection to each member of the Godhead is critical to living the life Jesus presented in the Bible. This book is written to help individuals remove lies and break hindrances that block God's gift of abundant life. Developing a way to achieve these goals has been Bethel Sozo's journey for the past twenty years.

Our desire is to provide you with the tools necessary for building a strong connection with God—one that remains unshakable in life's unpredictable storms. In this book, we will impart biblical tools that have the power to break lies, addictions, and hindrances over your life. This will connect you in a greater way to Father God, Jesus, and Holy Spirit and release you to walk powerfully in the call on your life.

Bethel Sozo is an inner healing and deliverance ministry. It provides a safe place for you to interact with God, which allows your heart to communicate openly with Him by supplanting lies with His truth to establish a powerful connection that lasts long after the Sozo session ends. Once you achieve this connection with the Father, Son, and Holy Spirit, you will be able to move past prior hindrances and achieve what Jesus came to earth to provide: the full Gospel.

An abundant life is something everyone desires. We are engineered to succeed, flourish, and live well. It is this God-given mandate to be fruitful and multiply that creates in us the capacity to change, improve, and overcome difficulties. Accessing this potential, however, does not simply happen. Living in the complete freedom Jesus purchased on the cross requires hard work, truth seeking, and fearless resolve.

This book is not intended to teach you how to provide a Sozo session. Its purpose is simply to give you a glimpse of what a Sozoed life looks like. If you are interested in pursuing the Sozo Ministry further, you can find resources online at www.bethelsozo.com.

Although this book is filled with useful information, it is your responsibility to practice the tools and see fruit develop. Thankfully, we serve a merciful God who encourages growth. By partnering with Him and practicing each principle presented, you will experience the abundant life Jesus provided through the cross.

Blessings,
Dawna and Teresa

WHAT DOES SOZO MEAN?

The Greek word *sōzō* is used over one hundred times in the New Testament. Its meanings are *to make well, heal, to restore to health, to keep safe, to deliver one from the penalties of the Messianic judgment, and to save from the evils which obstruct the reception of the Messianic deliverance.*[1]

The goal of the Bethel Sozo Ministry is to help individuals access these divine resources. We have found this can be accomplished, as our trust in God grows, through a strengthened connection with each member of the Godhead. This strengthened interaction with the Father, Son, and Holy Spirit helps identify the presence of lies and enemy strongholds in a person's life.

When people are held captive to a lie or stronghold, there can be harm to their physical, emotional, and spiritual health. To live in the freedom Christ demonstrated, individuals need to eradicate lies and/or demonic attachments and replace them with God's truth. As we will see later in this book, many biblical tools bring about this exchange.

While there are many fruitful inner healing ministries in the Body of Christ, Sozo has seen a substantial and increasing number of healings and testimonies around the world. This book will provide some examples of the breakthroughs we have seen. But first, let us look at some verses that show the biblical origins of Sozo.

The Sozo Ministry takes its name from the Greek word *sōzō*. The term, which we defined earlier, combines all three aspects of wholeness: salvation, healing, and deliverance. When the Bible uses *sōzō* to describe a person's breakthrough, the implication is that what is received is a full, three-dimensional blessing (one that includes physical, emotional, and spiritual health).

While no breakthrough should be seen as insignificant, at Bethel Sozo, we desire that our clients leave sessions whole. Anything less than wholeness falls short of Christ's gift of abundant life. We believe God's use of the word *sōzō* in Scripture is an invitation to experience not just salvation, healing, or deliverance, but all three.

The first time the Greek word *sōzō* appears is in Matthew 1:21:

> *She will give birth to a son, and you are to give Him the name Jesus, because He will **save** His people from their sins* (Matthew 1:21 NIV).

While translators use the word "save" for this particular passage, *sōzō*'s full definition implies all three facets of wholeness: *mak[ing] well, [salvation] from the evils which obstruct the reception of the Messianic deliverance*, and *[deliverance] from the penalties of the Messianic judgment*.[2] Jesus was not sent just to heal, save, or deliver. He was commissioned to do all three.

Some may ask: "What is the Messianic deliverance?" It is the freedom Jesus imparted through His death on the cross. By sacrificing His life for us, Christ saved humanity from sin, death, and eternal separation from God. Although lies and demonic obstructions can still hinder our walk (mostly through our allowing entry), Jesus reveals the truth that we are no longer slaves to their power (see Gal. 2:20). Sozo, as presented in Scripture, is God's process of removing hindrances that prevent us from walking fully in our redeemed life (see John 3:3).

In Matthew 9, translators use the word *sōzō* to describe a person's physical healing:

> *Just then a woman who had been subject to bleeding for twelve years came up behind Him and touched the edge of His cloak. She said to herself, "If I only touch His cloak, I will be* **healed***"* (Matthew 9:20-21 NIV).

Jesus tells the woman after this encounter, *"Take heart, daughter, your faith has healed you"* (Matt. 9:22 NIV). While translators use the word "healed," Scripture's use of the word *sōzō* signifies that the woman also experienced salvation and deliverance.

Scripture uses other words to indicate salvation, healing, or deliverance. *Sōzō* is the only one that combines all three. Other words for "saved" include *sōtēria*, which indicates a deliverance and salvation, and *pheugō*, which translates more as *fleeing away/saved by flight*.

Sōtēria is used 44 times in Scripture. Though the definition includes connotations of deliverance, *sōtēria* means specifically *the salvation of Christians for the benefit and blessing of salvation*.[3] The word itself communicates exclusivity.

Scripture uses this term during Jesus's interaction with the Samaritan woman:

> *You Samaritans worship what you do not know; we worship what we do know, for* **salvation** *is from the Jews* (John 4:22 NIV).

Jesus goes on to say there will be a time when true worshipers will honor the Father in spirit and truth, implying a spreading out of God's salvation gift (see John 4:23-24). Until then, salvation is reserved for

His people. The context of this verse implies a focus on salvation rather than a discussion about wholeness.

The word *pheugō* is used 29 times. It means *to flee away, seek safety by flight, to be saved by flight, and to escape safely out of danger*.[4] An example of this word is found in Mark:

> And they went out and **fled** from the tomb, for trembling and astonishment had seized them, and they said nothing to anyone, for they were afraid (Mark 16:8).

This word means *the physical action of removing oneself from harm*. Obviously, its use is quite different from *sōzō*'s and *sōtēria*'s.

The Bible also uses certain words to specify healing. These words include *iaomai*, *therapeuō*, and *diasōzō* (from *sōzō*). *Iaomai* is used 26 times in the New Testament. The definition is *to cure, heal, and to make whole (free from error and sins, to bring about one's salvation)*.[5] An example of *iaomai* occurs in Matthew 8:8,13:

> The centurion replied, "Lord, I do not deserve to have You come under my roof. But just say the word, and my servant will be healed." ...Then Jesus said to the centurion, "Go, it will be done just as you believed it would." And his servant was **healed** at that moment (Matthew 8:8,13 NIV).

Nothing in Scripture implies that anything more than physical healing took place. Regarding Scripture, we can only assume he received a physical healing while the woman who touched Jesus's cloak received wholeness.

The word *therapeuō* is used 43 times in Scripture. Its definition is *to serve, do service* and *to heal, cure, and restore to health*.[6] Translators use "heal" and "cure" more than "serve." An example of the word being used is first found in Matthew:

*Jesus rebuked the demon, and it came out of the boy, and he was **healed** [some use the word "cured"] at that moment* (Matthew 17:18 NIV).

While an obvious deliverance is taking place, one can see the emphasis of the passage is healing. There is no mention of salvation.

The term *diasōzō* is used nine times. Its roots extend from *sōzō* but carry the meanings of *preserving through danger, to bring safely through, and to keep from perishing.*[7] However, it can also be used as *to save, cure one who is sick, or bring him through:*

*And when the men of that place recognized Jesus, they sent word to all the surrounding country. People brought all their sick to Him and begged Him to let the sick just touch the edge of His cloak, and all who touched it were **healed*** (Matthew 14:35-36 NIV).

As we have seen, each of these words refers specifically to a physical healing rather than including salvation and deliverance.

Another word used specifically for deliverance, *aphesis*, is used 17 times in Scripture. The definition is *to be released from bondage or imprisonment or forgiveness or pardon as of sins.*[8] An example of this occurs in the following verse:

*John appeared, baptizing in the wilderness and proclaiming a baptism of repentance for the **forgiveness** of sins* (Mark 1:4).

Rather than focusing on healing or salvation, *aphesis* translates as *the release from sin's bondage.*

Whereas each of these words tailors specifically to concepts of healing, salvation, and deliverance, the word *sōzō* is the one that best combines all three. Sozo extends beyond physical healing and embraces the concept of spiritual, physical, and emotional wellness.

To better understand the difference between *sōzō* (*saved, healed, and delivered*) and other words like *iaomai* (specifically *healed*), examine this biblical story. It is helpful to note when Jesus uses each word:

> *While He was on the way to Jerusalem, He was passing between Samaria and Galilee. As He entered a village, ten leprous men who stood at a distance met Him; and they raised their voices, saying, "Jesus, Master, have mercy on us!" When He saw them, He said to them, "Go and show yourselves to the priests." And as they were going, they were cleansed. Now one of them, when he saw that he had been* **healed** *[iaomai], turned back, glorifying God with a loud voice, and he fell on his face at His feet, giving thanks to Him. And he was a Samaritan. Then Jesus answered and said, "Were there not ten cleansed? But the nine—where are they? Was no one found who returned to give glory to God, except this foreigner?" And He said to him, "Stand up and go; your faith has made you* **well** *[sōzō]"* (Luke 17:11-19 NASB).

Notice that of the ten lepers, only one received Jesus's full blessing. Because of his thankfulness, the leper accessed more of Heaven's gifts. While all ten of the lepers were healed, only one received a Sozo.

Some other verses that use the word *sōzō* are listed as follows:

> *But the one who endures to the end will be* **saved** (Matthew 24:13).

> *And Jesus said to him, "Go your way; your faith has made you* **well***." And immediately he recovered his sight and followed Him on the way* (Mark 10:52).

*The ones along the path are those who have heard; then the devil comes and takes away the word from their hearts, so that they may not believe and be **saved*** (Luke 8:12).

*And those who had seen it told them how the demon-possessed man had been **healed*** (Luke 8:36).

*For the Son of Man came to seek and to **save** the lost* (Luke 19:10).

*I am the door. If anyone enters by Me, he **will be saved** and will go in and out and find pasture* (John 10:9).

*If anyone hears My words and does not keep them, I do not judge him; for I did not come to judge the world but to **save** the world* (John 12:47).

*And it shall come to pass that everyone who calls upon the name of the Lord shall be **saved*** (Acts 2:21).

Replacing each italicized word or phrase with *sōzō* reflects the Lord's heart for wholesome deliverance. Jesus "did not come to judge the world but to save, heal, and deliver" it (see John 3:17; 12:47). He did not come to earth to see it partially saved. He came to give us everything.

In an effort to partner with God's desire of salvation, healing, and deliverance, Sozo aims to connect individuals to Heaven's truth. This is done by forming strong connections to each member of the Godhead. By discovering what the Father, Son, and Holy Spirit think of them, people are able to remove the lies that hinder their physical, spiritual, and emotional health.

We do not just want individuals physically healed; we also want them spiritually and emotionally restored like the sole leper who returned to Jesus. Like the *sōzōed* individuals in Scripture, we want people partnering with faith, approaching the Father, Son, and Holy Spirit, and communicating their physical, spiritual, and emotional needs.

Our ministry's goal is to allow individuals to receive Christ's full reward. Anything less is robbery.

NOTES

1. "Sozo" (4982). James Strong, *Strong's Exhaustive Concordance of the Bible,* 1981.

2. Ibid.

3. "Soteria" (4991). James Strong, *Strong's Exhaustive Concordance of the Bible*, 1981.

4. "Pheugo" (5343). James Strong, *Strong's Exhaustive Concordance of the Bible*, 1981.

5. "Iaomai" (2390). James Strong, *Strong's Exhaustive Concordance of the Bible*, 1981.

6. "Therapeuio" (2323). James Strong, *Strong's Exhaustive Concordance of the Bible*, 1981.

7. "Diasozo" (1295) from "Sozo" (4982). James Strong, *Strong's Exhaustive Concordance of the Bible*, 1981.

8. "Aphesis" (859) James Strong, *Strong's Exhaustive Concordance of the Bible,* 1981.

Chapter 1

BUILDING STRONG CONNECTIONS

It was a Sunday night in December 1997. Randy Clark, an international healing revivalist, had sent his trainer, Fred Grewe, to Bethel Church. Fred's desire was to train individuals on how to pray for attendees at the upcoming revival meeting. It was the height of winter in Redding, California. Bethel's congregation, well dressed for the cold, bundled themselves in coats, gloves, and hats. Fred stood at the pulpit overlooking the eager crowd.

Amongst those members were a few hungry, soon-to-be-influential inner healing ministers. They, however, did not realize it just yet. All Dawna and Teresa knew at that time was that they were tired of praying for people whose conditions did not improve. To learn more, Dawna and Teresa attended Fred's packed prayer servant training. If there was an answer, they were determined to find it.

As Fred spoke, he unveiled powerful inner healing tools. One such technique was Pablo Bottari's Ten Steps. This tool, originally used in the deliverance of new converts, would eventually be adapted to become a major pillar of the Sozo Ministry called the Four Doors.

Over the next two years, Dawna and Teresa continued to hone their skills. As they added tools, they began to notice their results improving. People were starting to get well and remain whole. Eventually, Beni Johnson, Bethel's prayer pastor, saw the ministry's fruit and gave her approval for Sozo to move forward under Dawna and Teresa's leadership.

Fast-forward 20 years. Dawna and Teresa's ministry has spread throughout the United States and the world. Establishing strong connections between individuals and the Godhead because of its ability to detect lies and exchange them for truth, Sozo has brought breakthrough to thousands.

Building strong connections is the foundation of Sozo. Everything taught—tools, techniques, and exercises—is aimed at connecting individuals to each member of the Godhead. This is because many Christians do not seem to easily access and relate to all three Persons of God. Many seem to only know Jesus on a surface level.

The Bible says God is One Being made up of three Persons: Father God, Jesus, and Holy Spirit. Throughout Scripture, we see each member of the Godhead providing specific needs. Whereas Father God tends to provide protection, provision, and identity, Jesus offers companionship and communication. The indwelling of the Holy Spirit provides comfort and instruction.

We have found that living a powerful life as Christians is directly linked to how well we steward our relationships with the Godhead. Empowered people are those who bring their needs before the Father, Son, and Holy Spirit. Those who connect to Father God receive identity and purpose. Those who communicate with Jesus receive companionship. Those who partner with the Holy Spirit receive instruction and comfort. This model closely mirrors the relationships within the human family. Healthy mothers, fathers, siblings, and friends each contribute to a person's physical, emotional, and spiritual growth. (The Father Ladder, a tool that explores this concept, will be discussed later.)

We believe that those who fail to pursue Father God, Jesus, and Holy Spirit individually reduce their impact on the world because they fail to access this relationship that provides identity, purpose, relationship, and comfort.

Most, if not all, Christians are comfortable with Jesus. However, their level of relationship with Him may need some improvement. Many Christians, especially in Western nations, lack deep relationships with Jesus, Holy Spirit, or Father God. This is because religion, rather than relationship, takes the place of importance.

This is one reason why we believe the Church often sits on the sidelines of today's culture. Whether from fear or inconvenience, many Christians fail to pursue a personal relationship with God. Without a passion for and a close companionship with the Godhead, their ability to influence others is decreased. Like the covered lamp in Jesus's parable, they are unable to function as designed:

> *You are the salt of the earth, but if salt has lost its taste, how shall its saltiness be restored? It is no longer good for anything except to be thrown out and trampled under people's feet. You are the light of the world. A city set on a hill cannot be hidden. Nor do people light a lamp and put it under a basket, but on a stand, and it gives light to all in the house. In the same way, let your light shine before others, so that they may see your good works and give glory to your Father who is in heaven (Matthew 5:13-16).*

An important purpose of our lives is to bring light and influence others. When we reduce our ability to give light, we diminish our capacity to shape nations.

The world benefits when Christians become healthy. When they build a strong connection with God, believers are empowered to live the way Jesus demonstrated. They know who they are and what they were born for, and they realize that they have an unbreakable connection that will not fail them in moments of testing.

We have found that in order to build connections with each member of the Godhead, we must identify the hindrances that have damaged our ability to trust God. Usually the issue involves partnering with a lie, wound, or ungodly mindset. Doing this opens doors to ungodly behaviors and possible demonic oppression.

Lies tend to be the most common hindrance to a person's connection with God. Because of childhood hurts, traumas, and other negative experiences, a person may develop false conclusions about people and God. For instance, children who experience divorce often blame themselves for their parents' separation. This, obviously, is not the truth, and the assumption must be renounced for the person to break free from the power of this belief.

No matter how ridiculous a lie or false belief sounds, a person may partner with it if it helps him rationalize his situation. Often lies are so ingrained that it takes partnership with the Holy Spirit to reveal their presence. This is why Paul urges believers to renew their minds:

> *Do not be conformed to this world, but be transformed by the renewal of your mind, that by testing you may discern what is the will of God, what is good and acceptable and perfect* (Romans 12:2).

Until our minds are renewed, we struggle with mentalities that are in opposition to God. Sozo sessions confront this opposition by replacing lies with God's truth.

To better understand the process of Sozo sessions, here is a typical opening conversation:

(Sozo minister and client enter room and sit.)

Sozo minister: "How are you doing today?"

Client: "Fine."

Sozo minister: "What is it you would like prayer for?"

Client: "I'd like to have a stronger connection with the Holy Spirit."

Sozo minister: "Is there any reason in particular?"

Client: "No, I've just never really gotten into it. My friends say they have a great relationship with the Holy Spirit, but I don't."

Sozo minister: "We can work on that. Why don't you close your eyes? Just so it will be easier to focus."

Client: "Okay." *(Closes eyes)*

Sozo minister: "When you think about the Holy Spirit, what do you hear, feel, or see?"

Client: *(Tries to picture Holy Spirit)*

Sozo minister: "Are you seeing, sensing, or hearing anything?"

Client: "No."

Sozo minister: "All right. Repeat after me: 'I renounce the lie that I am unable to hear, see, or sense the Holy Spirit. I renounce the lie that He does not want to talk with me. I break off any blockages to You in Jesus's name. Holy Spirit, would You reveal Yourself to me?'"

Client: *(Repeats prayer)*

Sozo minister: *(Waits until he or she feels client is ready)* "What do you hear, sense, or see?"

Notice how in this scenario the Sozo minister asked the client to close his eyes and relate how he connects with the Holy Spirit. This is a common practice in Sozo sessions. Ministers tend to work with a person's pictures, feelings, thoughts, senses, or impressions. This is because God communicates uniquely with each individual. Some people see pictures more easily, while others more readily feel God's presence. To respect each person's way of sensing His presence, Sozo ministers give clients the freedom to encounter God through whichever method He chooses.

Sometimes clients are unable to hear, see, or sense anything. We have found this always to be the result of a lie, wound, or other hindrance from the enemy. When this occurs, we work with the client through prayer to discover the root of the problem. (The tools we use to help with this will be discussed at length in later chapters.)

As Sozo ministers, our job is never to judge how a person thinks, sees, or feels God. Our job is to take whatever information the client gives us and discover the presence of lies that hinder the development of a strong connection with the Lord. If he or she is willing to renounce ties with any lies, strongholds, and destructive patterns, ministers can work through forgiveness, renunciation, and other Sozo tools to remove each negative presence.

As seen in the example above, connecting to a member of the Godhead follows a simple process. By asking people how they sense, see, or hear God, Sozo ministers are able to discern which lies hinder that person's connection to the Lord.

For example, a person who sees the Holy Spirit as a mist or unclear substance might believe the lie that the Holy Spirit is unavailable. He or she may believe the Holy Spirit is only a spiritual substance and not a Person desiring an intimate relationship. The Bible is clear in its representation of the Holy Spirit as a real, living, and powerful Being.

One of the most powerful tools in Sozo, which we will go over later, is called the *Father Ladder*. By mapping out our emotional, physical, and spiritual needs, the Father Ladder helps to chart out which relationships of the Godhead need strengthening. For instance, if the need for comfort is not getting met, establishing a stronger relationship with the Holy Spirit will open the door to His fulfilling that need.

Working through the Father Ladder, Sozo ministers discover which human relationships the person needs to forgive, if any. This could be a mother, father, friend, or anyone else he has held offense against, including himself or herself. The reason Sozo ministers use forgiveness is that the release of offense frees people to receive God's blessing. This biblical principle found in Matthew 18 is used even in medical psychology (known as Forgiveness Therapy). When a person relinquishes his hate or judgment of another person, physical, emotional, and spiritual healing takes place.

Once again, the main goal for any successful Sozo session is to build a strong connection between an individual and each member of the Godhead. Because relationship with Father God, Jesus, and Holy Spirit gives us our true identity and provides protection, communication, and comfort, it is crucial that we establish a strong connection with each member so that we can weather life's storms.

At the end of each chapter, a series of activation questions are included. Partner with the Holy Spirit as you work through them. Write down what He says and walk through the activation process by yourself or with a group leader.

| Group Discussion Questions |

1. Out of the three members of the Godhead, is there a particular member to whom you feel closest?

2. If there were anything you could get out of having a personal relationship with Jesus, Father God, or Holy Spirit, what would it be?

| Activation |

1. Choose a member of the Godhead you wish to strengthen your relationship with: Father God, Jesus, or the Holy Spirit. Ask whomever you choose if there is a lie you are believing about Him.

2. Ask Father God, Jesus, or the Holy Spirit where you learned this lie.

3. Ask Father God, Jesus, or the Holy Spirit to show you where He was in that moment.

4. Ask Father God, Jesus, or the Holy Spirit to reveal the truth of the situation.

5. Release forgiveness to anyone who taught you to partner with this specific lie.

6. Hand to God, Jesus, or the Holy Spirit any demonic attachments or ungodly mindsets that grew from this event.

7. Ask God, Jesus, or the Holy Spirit to replace the lie with His truth.

Conclusion

After working through the activation exercises and group discussions, reflect on what Father God, Jesus, or Holy Spirit revealed. Ponder His words. Thank Him for whatever breakthrough you experience.

| Suggested Materials |

Matthew 18:21-35

Johnson, Bill. *Face to Face with God: The Ultimate Quest to Experience His Presence.* Lake Mary, FL: Charisma House, 2007. Print.

Vallotton, Jason. *The Supernatural Power of Forgiveness: Discover How to Escape Your Prison of Pain and Unlock a Life of Freedom.* Bloomington, MN: Chosen Books, 2011. Print.

Chapter 2

JESUS AS FRIEND AND MEDIATOR

Could the ministry team please step to the front?" Pastor Bill Johnson motioned his prayer servants forward. Dawna made her way to the stage. Halfway through the ministry time, a middle-aged man named Daniel came forward and introduced himself. Dawna asked why he needed prayer. Daniel replied, "Deliverance."

As they worked through issues, Daniel confessed that as a teenager he had sold his soul to the devil. Surprised, but not wanting to appear too concerned, Dawna held her non-shocked "Sozo face" and asked, "Why?" With tears in his eyes, Daniel explained.

As far back as Daniel could remember, his dad had been a violent drunk. One night, when Daniel was 14, his dad had come home from work completely intoxicated. Daniel raced to his bedroom to hide beneath the sheets. He could hear his dad rampaging throughout the house.

Terrified, Daniel clutched the bedsheets and asked Jesus if He were real, to appear and save his family. Seeing no immediate change, Daniel asked satan if he were real, to rescue his family. Within seconds, a demonic presence filled the room. Terrified, Daniel promised his soul if only it would keep his family safe.

At 16, Daniel ran away from home and entered into a life of drugs. Not until he overdosed at the age of 18 was he again visited by the demonic entity. This time it told Daniel that his time was up. In a sort of post-death vision, Daniel saw himself outside of his body and cried out to Jesus for help. Immediately, Jesus appeared. Daniel's overdose ended. He woke up on the floor of his apartment completely free from drug addiction. Afterward, he gave his heart to Jesus. Following this encounter, Daniel started attending church. However, he sensed the demonic spirit was still attached to his life.

Fifteen years later, Daniel sobbed at the prayer line. Seeing the guilt left from his past sin, Dawna gently asked if Daniel wanted to speak to Jesus about this specific memory. Through sobs, Daniel said, "Yes."

Dawna led him through a prayer of forgiveness, "Close your eyes. Repeat after me: 'Jesus, I ask You to forgive me for creating an unhealthy soul tie with the demonic realm. I renounce the lie that even though I am with You, I still have to be bound to its presence. Jesus, what do You have for me in exchange?'"

Daniel repeated the prayer.

Dawna continued, "What do you see, sense, or hear?"

Daniel cocked his head as if listening to an interior conversation. "I don't know. Jesus wants to tell me something, but I can't quite hear Him."

"Repeat after me: 'Jesus, would You show me where You were in that moment when I first cried out for Your safety?'"

Daniel replied, "I saw myself as a boy hiding under the sheets in my bedroom. But this time, Jesus showed up. He was so huge that He filled the entire room."

"How does that make you feel?"

"Kind of dumb. I wish I had seen Him."

"Repeat after me: 'Jesus, thank You for revealing Yourself to me in that memory. I ask You to forgive me for not noticing when You entered the room. I renounce the lie that You are angry with me for not recognizing Your presence. I give You permission, Jesus, to teach me how to recognize when You come near.

Daniel finished the prayer.

Dawna leaned forward, "How does that make you feel?"

Daniel opened his eyes. A grin formed across his face. "Thank You, Jesus."

Daniel's voice cracked. He doubled over into a succession of sobs. When she felt he was ready, Dawna continued.

"Repeat after me: 'Jesus, thank You for revealing Yourself to me. I renounce the lie that my soul, at any time, belonged to the enemy. I hand this lie to You in Jesus's name and ask that You would cleanse me from any and all ties to the demonic realm. I ask this all in Jesus's name. Jesus, what do You have for me in exchange?'"

Dawna waited to hear Daniel's response.

"What do you hear, sense, or see?"

Daniel wiped his eyes with the back of each wrist.

"Jesus said He is proud of me. I saw Him rip the document that I had signed to the devil. Then He gave me a new contract and said I'm now in partnership with Him."

"How does that make you feel?"

"Pretty good."

"Repeat after me: 'Thank You, Jesus, for tearing this false document. I separate myself from all of its ties and hand You each piece. I ask, Jesus, that You would preserve me with Your blessing. I seal these truths in Your Holy name. Amen.'"

Daniel repeated the prayer. Drying his eyes, he looked at Dawna and gave her a massive bear hug.

In a powerful act of exchange, Daniel severed partnership with the enemy and established a covenant with Jesus.

Jesus fulfills many roles for us throughout our lives. However, there are two main characteristics Sozo ministers focus on when reconnecting individuals to Christ, that of *friend* and *mediator*.

Everyone who has received Jesus understands to some extent *Jehovah-Tsidkenu*, "the Lord our righteousness." To accept His calling, each of us had to let go of opposing mindsets. It is a trade-off every believer experiences. To receive eternity, we must first be willing to remove the obstacles that block His entry (see Rev. 3:20).

This process of removal stands at the core of all Sozo sessions. To receive God's truth, individuals must follow a process of *identification*, *renunciation*, *forgiveness*, and *exchange*. Each of these steps helps to identify the enemy's fingerprints and works to replace them with God's truth.

The first role Sozo ministers investigate with a person is Jesus's function as our *friend*. While the significance of this concept may be diluted in contemporary society, understanding this relationship has the power to shape nations. Jesus was, is, and is eternally God (see John 1:1-14). Having relationship with Him means we have relationship with the Father.

As God, Jesus represents the greatest friendship we can ever experience. Forsaking Himself, He gave us the ultimate gift, redemption through His sacrifice:

> *Greater love has no one than this, that someone lay down his life for his friends* (John 15:13).

Jesus acted as our ultimate friend by surrendering His life so ours could be eternal.

In Western cultures, the concept of friendship rarely encompasses this level of devotion. Most people form friendships based on how they are treated. When a person feels accepted, he often pursues that new, safe relationship. Jesus's method, however, works differently. He chooses relationship regardless of whether we like Him or not. This radical act gives us permission either to accept or reject His offer.

Either way, as believers, once we accept His gift of the cross, we are marked by His love:

For I am sure that neither death nor life, nor angels nor rulers, nor things present nor things to come, nor powers, nor height nor depth, nor anything else in all creation, will be able to separate us from the love of God in Christ Jesus our Lord (Romans 8:38-39).

We have the capacity to choose friendship with the One who never leaves, rejects, or disappoints. The perfect representation of the Father, Jesus acts as our closest friend. When others reject us, Jesus does not. All we have to do to access this friendship is to open our hearts:

Behold, I stand at the door and knock. If anyone hears My voice and opens the door, I will come in to him and eat with him, and he with Me (Revelation 3:20).

While on earth, Jesus demonstrated His friendship by communicating directly with His disciples. He involved them in His Father's plans. Jesus acted as the perfect communicator:

No longer do I call you servants, for the servant does not know what his master is doing; but I have called you friends, for all that I have heard from My Father I have made known to you (John 15:15).

The Bible also tells us that Jesus was and is our older sibling. By making Himself lower than the angels, Jesus underwent human incarnation so that He could atone for humanity's sins:

Therefore He had to be made like His brothers in every respect, so that He might become a merciful and faithful high priest in the service of God, to make propitiation for the sins of the people (Hebrews 2:17).

Because Jesus experienced an actual physical existence, He can relate to any and every situation we face.

As the younger siblings of Jesus, we have the capacity to access all that He owns. This is what Christ's death provided—adoption into God's Kingdom and full access to Heaven's resources. Paul expands on this relationship by stating that we humans are children of God:

The Spirit Himself bears witness with our spirit that we are children of God, and if children, then heirs—heirs of God and fellow heirs with Christ, provided we suffer with Him in order that we may also be glorified with Him (Romans 8:16-17).

Paul claims that as children of God we become co-heirs of His Kingdom. Partnering with His promise, we gain access to Heaven's domain. This is why we can "boldly go before the throne of grace" (see Heb. 4:16). We are not simply visiting the Throne Room—we belong there.

Also noted in Scripture is Jesus's second major role in our lives as our perfect *mediator*. Paul states:

Who is to condemn? Christ Jesus is the one who died—more than that, who was raised—who is at the right hand of God, who indeed is interceding for us (Romans 8:34).

Jesus intercedes for us continuously. He has our best interests at heart. In light of this, it is not surprising to see that many Christians relate to Jesus better than the other two members of the Godhead. Of the Trinity, Jesus generally is seen as the most personable and easiest to relate to. Because of the ease with which we relate to Jesus, we often begin Sozo sessions with Him.

Guided by Scripture, Sozo presents Jesus as our savior, friend, and mediator. In these roles, Christ meets our spiritual and emotional needs as well as our need for *companionship* and *communication*.

Our human relationships with friends and siblings closely mirror our relationship with Jesus. Friends and siblings, like Jesus, fulfill our need of communication and companionship. Because of this, when issues arise in these areas, clients must connect with Jesus to meet these needs. (All of this is outlined in the Father Ladder tool, which will be discussed later.) Sozo ministers find that strained relationships with friends or siblings lead to skewed views of Jesus.

This is not to say that people will consciously block off Jesus after being let down by a friend. It is to state that as humans, we tend to transpose hurts onto others in order to avoid pain. When a friend or sibling fails to supply a need, we may build a wall against that person who caused offense. This becomes an issue when we unconsciously build a wall between ourselves and Jesus.

As children, we learn to communicate, build trust, and form relationships through friends and siblings. These relationships create in us an expectation for how we interact with Jesus. Either we see Him as a safe place of connection, communication, and growth or as a dysfunctional area in need of attention. Our relationship with Him is affected by whether or not we have had good connections with our friends and siblings growing up.

When a friend or sibling hurts our feelings, especially in our formative years, there is a chance that a lie from the enemy can develop. Resolving this issue in a safe environment can remove destructive patterns that seek to interrupt God's purpose.

Take, for example, James, an older gentleman who scheduled an appointment through Bethel Redding's Sozo Transformation Center. Having been on his own for some time, James entered Sue's office carrying a heavy burden. Though he did not speak of his pain aloud, she could pick up on his "sorrowful atmosphere" (more on that later).

After spending a few minutes in discussion, Sue discovered the reason for much of James's pain. As a boy, James had watched his younger sibling, Drew, descend into a spiral of depression. Unable to connect to his brother emotionally, James blamed himself for his brother's suicide at the age of 16. Although clearly not responsible for his brother's death, James could not shake his feelings of guilt.

Unfortunately, James carried this guilt throughout life. Not until now, in his late 60s, did he seek release. The first step he worked through was forgiveness. His feelings, long internalized, had grown to such a depth that they colored the way he saw himself and God. His unwillingness to move past fear and self-pity stunted his growth.

Sue asked James why he found it so difficult to release himself from judgment.

"Jesus wouldn't forgive me," he said.

"How do you know?"

"How could He? I let my brother die."

"Do you want to ask Jesus and see what He thinks?"

"I already know what He thinks."

"Why don't we ask Jesus, anyway? If you're right, we'll move on with the rest of the session. If you're wrong, you may experience breakthrough."

Let us take a moment to step out of this session and see what is going on. We have found that giving Sozo clients options is very effective. When conducting a session, we do not follow our own agendas to prove a client's mindsets are incorrect. Instead, by facilitating a safe conversation with God, Sozo sessions reflect His desired process for growth. This dedication to the Lord's will is modeled in Jesus's life:

> So Jesus said to them, "Truly, truly, I say to you, the Son can do nothing of His own accord, but only what He sees the Father doing. For whatever the Father does, that the Son does likewise" (John 5:19).

Now, let us return to the session.

With some reluctance, James agreed to meet with Jesus.

"Close your eyes. I'm going to ask you to remember a time when you tried to comfort your brother."

James took a moment before deciding.

"If it becomes too much, we can move on. For now, I want you to close your eyes and revisit that specific memory. Are you there?"

James nodded. He quietly admitted that he had relived such memories nearly every day of his life since the death occurred.

"Repeat after me: 'Jesus, would You show me where You were in this memory?'"

As if on cue, James doubled over. Sue slid a box of tissue beside his feet. Careful not to interrupt, she sat in silent intercession. (She did not want to distract James and keep him from encountering Jesus.) After several minutes, Sue asked James what he experienced. James opened his eyes. He pulled a tissue from the box.

"I saw Drew. He and Jesus were standing in the cafeteria of our old school. Drew always liked the food. After his death, my family pulled me out of the school and taught me at home."

He paused. "I'm remembering when they took Drew's body away by ambulance. As the medics lifted his body, Jesus embraced me and said it wasn't my fault."

James sunk in his seat. A moment of silence followed.

"How does that make you feel?" Sue asked.

James wiped his eyes. "I guess it's time to move on and let Drew be with Jesus."

"Are you ready to do that?"

"I think so."

"Repeat after me: 'I choose to forgive myself for not preventing my brother's suicide. I ask You to forgive me, Jesus, for placing unhealthy guilt and responsibility on my life. I release myself from all self-judgment and I release my brother in Jesus's name. Amen.'"

James repeated the prayer. Tears glistened on his cheeks.

"How do you feel?"

"Light. For the first time in 50 years."

"Let's take some time to thank Jesus and see if we need to work on anything else. Does that sound good?"

"Sounds great."

James wiped his face. After making sure he was ready to progress, Sue continued the session.

As exemplified with James, forgiveness plays an important role in a person's healing. Forgiveness is one of Heaven's most powerful weapons. Jesus explains its significance in the Book of Matthew:

> *Then his master summoned him and said to him, 'You wicked servant! I forgave you all that debt because you pleaded with me. And should not you have had mercy on your fellow servant, as I had mercy on you?' And in anger his master delivered him to the jailers, until he should pay all his debt. So also My Heavenly Father will do to every one of you, if you do not forgive your brother from your heart* (Matthew 18:32-35).

This is a powerfully clear verse showing how unforgiveness (even toward ourselves) locks us away in a prison where the key to the lock is simply to forgive. In Ephesians, Paul shows us some of the benefits of this key:

> *Let all bitterness and wrath and anger and clamor and slander be away from you, along with all malice. Be kind to one another, tenderhearted, forgiving one another, as God in Christ forgave you* (Ephesians 4:31-32).

Forgiveness is the key that enables us to walk away from bitterness and other opposing spirits. Accepting God's forgiveness of us through Christ means that we are not stuck in a mindset of guilt and shame.

We have often found that guilt and shame are common roadblocks to a person's healing.

Because of the void left by his deceased brother, James had trouble connecting with Jesus as the friend who is "closer than a brother" (see Prov. 18:24). Because of his brother's loss, he had a strained concept of a relationship with Christ. He appreciated the idea of Christ being a companion; however, when it came to practical application, Christ remained an abstract idea. To help solve this issue, James needed a personal encounter with Jesus—something that would show that Christ was there with James at the place of his original wounds.

James needed to see Jesus in his painful memory. We use this technique often in Sozo sessions. This tool, called *Presenting Jesus*, is used to find where lies originated in the person's life. After discovering a lie's origin, clients ask Jesus to reveal Himself and impart His truth about the event or memory. Although we believe that not everyone needs to revisit past memories, some of the greatest breakthroughs in Sozo have developed from this tool.

James needed to see Jesus as a friend and savior in the midst of suffering. By allowing Jesus to take responsibility for Drew, James was able to let go and experience freedom.

Notice that in James's session, Jesus served both as a communicator and companion. By meeting with James in the midst of the painful memory, Jesus was able to communicate truth. As the perfect communicator, Jesus assured James that his brother's death was not his fault. Although tragedy had taken Drew's life, Jesus showed James that he was not alone in coping with this hurt. Jesus had been there, too—like a friend closer than a brother (see Prov. 18:24). This released James from the pain of being a failed protector. When Jesus imparted forgiveness, all blame tied to his brother's suicide was instantly eradicated.

James finally realized that Jesus did not blame him for Drew's death. Therefore, he did not need to blame himself. This was the beginning step James needed in order to move forward emotionally and spiritually in his life—to leave behind the burden of regret.

Not all wounds we carry in our relationship to Jesus are so traumatic. Any lies the enemy uses to deceive us regarding our friendships and siblings can cause distance between us and Jesus. Jesus relates to each person in a unique and personal way. Consider this story about Dawna's son, Cory.

Cory was in the sixth grade when this event occurred. He had always been small as a child and was substantially shorter than other children of his age at this time. During the morning recess, an eighth grader called out to him across the playground: "Hey, I thought all the pre-k students went home after recess." Obviously, this left a painful mark.

Several hours later, Cory sat in the library with other students working with a teacher's aide for extra help in math. Dawna, whose office was next to the library, would often join the teacher's aide to help these students with their math skills. On this day, however, as Cory opened his math book, he began to softly cry. When Dawna asked what was wrong, he was unable to explain his sadness. He instead asked if they could do that "Sozo thing" she did.

Dawna signed him out from school and headed to the parking lot. While starting the car and pulling out, Dawna asked, "What's up, sweetie?"

"I don't know."

"What happened?"

"I was at recess and this eighth grader said he thought all the pre-k students had already gone home."

"I'm so sorry, bud. Why don't you close your eyes? Let's see what Jesus wants to show you."

Cory closed his eyes and replayed the memory.

"Ask Jesus to show you where He was in that picture."

"He's standing near Kelly."

At this point Dawna's first reaction was to think, *Jesus, why are You standing with that bully?* Instead of reacting out loud, Dawna asked Cory what lie Kelly taught him in that memory.

After asking Jesus what lie he had learned, Cory opened his eyes, "That I'm a momma's boy."

"Jesus, what is the truth?"

Cory asked the question and laughed at the answer he received. "Jesus wouldn't say that, would He?"

"What did you hear?"

"Jesus said, 'Don't worry, Kelly was just being stupid.'"

What a fun example of Jesus as our friend. Jesus spoke to Cory at his age level, similar to the way his friends would have encouraged him. This possibly hurtful situation could have planted a seed for Cory to believe that he was not sufficient enough on his own and was too protected. Instead, the lie was quickly scooped up and dispelled by truth. It would be beneficial to note, however, that upon returning to class, Dawna cautioned Cory not to tell Kelly that Jesus thought he was stupid.

This is why it is so helpful to minister to children through Sozo. When these lies are seen through the lens of Jesus's truth, the power for them to grow into damaging mindsets is averted. Years later, when Dawna shared this in a Sozo seminar that Cory attended, he told her he did not even remember that event occurring. This was further evidence that healing had taken place in Cory with this quick exchange of prayer.

It is rewarding to watch Jesus bring truth into places of pain. Over and over, we see Jesus heal hurts, remove lies, and exchange those lies for truths. Connecting people to Jesus as a friend, companion, and savior opens the way to clearer communication between themselves and God.

In examining your own life, are there areas with your friends and siblings that need prayer and breakthrough? Maybe you need to work through forgiveness with your friends? Perhaps your friend or sibling did not show you honor growing up? Do you feel a never-ending sense of loneliness even when surrounded by people who say they love you? Chances are there are some lies that need to be dealt with.

Healing happens because those hungry enough to seek it out are brave enough to confront their fears. To help you do some searching of your own, we have provided the following questions. Do these alone or with a trusted spiritual authority.

| Group Discussion Questions |

1. Is there a place of awkwardness or distance between you and your siblings?

2. Do you find it hard to connect with people your own age?

| Activation |

Lies About Yourself

1. Ask Jesus to reveal to you if you are believing a lie about yourself.

2. Ask Jesus where you learned this lie.

3. Ask Him to show you where He was in that moment.

4. Ask Him to reveal the truth of the situation.

5. Release forgiveness to anyone who taught you this lie or caused you harm in this memory.

6. Hand to Jesus any demonic attachments or ungodly mindsets that came about because of this event.

7. Ask Him to replace the mindsets with truth and to take up the space vacated by any demonic attachments with more of His daily presence.

Lies About Jesus

1. Ask Jesus to reveal to you if you are believing a lie about Him.

2. Ask Him where you learned this lie.

3. Ask Him to show you where He was in that moment.

4. Ask Him to reveal the truth of the situation.

5. Release forgiveness to anyone who taught you this lie or caused you harm in this memory.

6. Ask Jesus to forgive you for believing this lie about Him. Renounce the lie and hand to Him any demonic attachments or ungodly mindsets that came about because of this event.

7. Ask Him to replace these mindsets with truth and to take up the space vacated by any demonic influences with more of His daily presence.

| Suggested Materials |

Arthur, Kay. Lord, *I Want to Know You: A Devotional Study on the Names of God*. Colorado Springs: Waterbrook Press, 1933. Print.

The Gospels: Matthew, Mark, Luke, John

Chapter 3

STOPPING AT THE DOOR OF JESUS

Picture yourself standing in a dark room. A beam of light illuminates the knob of a red door. You walk toward it, uncertain of what lies behind. Reluctant at first, you test the knob. It turns. Slowly, the door opens.

You enter a brightly lit room. Inside you see three doors. The one on the left says, "Christ." It opens. Radiant light splashes your eyes. After your pupils adjust, you recognize the Savior, Jesus, opening His arms to offer you salvation and abundant life. There is a knowing inside of you as you approach that you are stepping into a living, vibrant friendship:

> *No longer do I call you servants, for the servant does not know what his master is doing; but I have called you friends, for all that I have heard from My Father I have made known to you* (John 15:15).

After a few years of building trust with you, Jesus invites you back into the outer room. At first you hesitate, but this place with Jesus has become so comfortable. You have learned to cherish the time spent here and wonder if that will change once leaving this room.

Hesitant, you follow Jesus into the outer room where a second, much broader door awaits. Its knob, made of gold, bears the insignia of a lion. You feel as though a powerful presence resides behind its frame.

Jesus asks if you would like to enter. You contemplate at first, then reach for the handle. Inside are white light, thunder, and the crack of earthquakes.

As your eyes adjust, you see a throne. On it sits an ominous figure, the size of a city, eyes alive and sharp. Your eyes meet. For a second, you feel safe. However, safety soon melts to fear as you gaze into the eyes of a presence too great to comprehend.

With a scream, you shut the door. Jesus asks if you would like to go back inside. You shake your head and suggest returning to Jesus's room.

"We've already been there," Jesus says. "Wouldn't you like to see the Father?"

"Maybe later."

Jesus follows you back to His room. In His domain, you feel safe. This place, which transitioned you from death to life, fills your heart with promise. Why would you ever want to give that up?

Does any of this sound familiar? Although presented as an allegory, it is a good illustration of the average Christian life. Like the protagonist, many believers embrace Christ's sacrifice yet fail to access relationships with the Father and the Holy Spirit. As Stephen De Silva, CFO of Bethel Church, states, "Many Christians stop at the door of Jesus because of fears, doubts, and insecurities. Doing this, they fail to access the Father."

This is a major issue today in a world filled with people who partner with an orphan mentality. Those who grew up with absent fathers or strained paternal relationships often inherently believe they are lost, alone, and needing to perform for love and approval. Acting out of these beliefs, they distort Christ's empowering message.

People who do not know God as the ultimate, loving Father usually have trouble believing in His *protection*, *provision*, and impartation of *identity*. Likewise, those who ignore relationship with the Holy Spirit deny themselves the gifts of being *nurtured, instructed,* and *comforted.* When we do not allow God to meet these needs, our spiritual, physical, and emotional health can be stunted.

The chief objective of the orphan mindset is to distance a person from God. Its lies keep a person from seeking a personal relationship with the Father. To remedy this, Christ's spirit of adoption, which closes the gap by introducing the Father's heart, must be accessed. (See Romans 8:15).

Breaking off the orphan mindset is one goal of a Sozo experience. Restoring relationship to each of the three members of the Godhead is key to ensuring this takes place. If Sozo ministers can help people connect relationally with each of God's aspects, these fears, which hinder us from living powerfully, will be rendered obsolete.

Bill Johnson, senior leader of Bethel Church in Redding, points out, "A single encounter with the Lord can change a lifetime's work of fear. His heart is really that good."

During one Sozo teaching, Dawna prayed for a young woman to connect her heart to the Father. A man sitting in the row behind named Jim began to cry. Jim had come to the seminar as a requirement of his AA weekend. Arriving with several friends on motorcycles, he had basketball-sized muscles and cultic tattoos covering his arms. When Dawna finished praying for the woman, she noticed Jim's tears and asked what was happening.

Jim answered, "I've got this Jesus thing down. I love Him, and I know He loves me. But this Father God thing, I have no idea what you're talking about."

"So," Dawna said. "You feel safe with Jesus?"

"He and I are great," Jim said. "But this Father thing doesn't make sense."

"Would you be willing to ask Jesus to take you to His Father?"

"I'll try," Jim said and closed his eyes.

"Repeat after me: 'Jesus, would You take me to Your Father?'"

After praying this, Jim shielded his face as if avoiding a strike.

Seeing this, Dawna leaned in close to Jim's ear and whispered, "Father God will never strike you."

At this, Jim collapsed. Sobbing, he drew his legs to his chest and held himself in a fetal position. Detecting a possible demonic manifestation, Dawna knelt beside him and asked him if this was a good or bad cry.

Through groans, Jim confessed, "Father God is holding me." Here Dawna commanded all demonic attachments to the mindsets of rage, hatred, abuse, and fear to leave Jim. As Jim calmed down, for the first time in his life he experienced the safety of a father.

Jim left his encounter a completely different person. Having carried around the lie that he was an orphan his entire life, Jim now had the ability to see himself as a loved and protected son. This was something he never experienced as a child. As Jim later disclosed, his father, when present, would beat him mercilessly. It was only when he ran away from home at the age of 16 that he felt any sort of freedom. Now, at 40 plus years old, Jim experienced a re-engineering of his life. The Father's unconditional love was revealed and accepted.

Not all exchanges with the Father end this way. A person's wounds can be so traumatic that additional encounters are required. In these instances, it is important to remember that God has each of His sons and daughters on a timeline. He knows when and how best to give us an encounter.

This was the case for a young woman named Kim who attended a Sozo conference in the midst of a financial crisis. Her husband, with whom she had been jointly operating their successful business, had just confessed to siphoning funds for the last 17 years. As police were getting involved, Kim decided to fly out to attend the meeting.

After the conference's opening session, Kim came to the front and asked for prayer.

"What is it you want prayer for today?" Carol, the trainer, asked.

"It's about my husband, Jerry. We've been married 40 years. Six days ago, I found out he'd been stealing from our business. Now the police are after him, and I don't know what to do."

Finding a piece of tissue and offering it to Kim, Carol asked, "What is it that you want prayer for?"

"I want to forgive my husband, but he lied to me for 17 years. How can someone forgive that?"

"Let's ask Jesus what He thinks about the situation."

Kim nodded and dried her cheeks.

"Jesus, what do you think about me and my situation?"

After repeating the prayer, Kim's eyes tightened.

"What do you hear, sense, or see?"

"Jesus said He's sorry, that He never wanted this to happen."

"How does that make you feel?"

"Good. But why did this have to happen? Couldn't He have stopped it?"

"Let's ask. Jesus, why did this happen?"

Kim dabbed the corner of her eyes.

"What did you hear, sense, or see?"

"Nothing. All I see is a dark, empty landscape."

"How does it make you feel?"

"Sad."

"Repeat after me: 'I choose to forgive my husband for lying to me all these years, and I forgive any of my friends and family members for abandoning me in moments of crisis. I renounce the lie that I am alone. I hand You this lie, Jesus. What truth do You have in exchange for me?'"

After waiting several seconds, Carol asked, "What do you hear, sense, or see?"

"I see my friends, those who abandoned me in the dark periods of my life. I see my husband standing apart from the rest. He's got his arm raised as if waving good-bye."

"Repeat after me: 'I choose to forgive my friends for abandoning me in dark seasons. For running away in times of loss when I needed them most. And I choose to forgive my husband, who made me trust his intentions while practicing deceit. I forgive him for bringing dishonesty into our marriage. Jesus, as I forgive him, what would You like to give me in exchange?'"

Kim wiped tears from her eyes.

"What do you hear, sense, or see?"

"I see Jesus with His arms around my husband. They are going away together. I don't know where. But I feel peace."

"Jesus, can I trust You to take care of my husband? Can I trust You to keep him safe?"

Kim repeated the prayer. "Yes. But will God keep me safe? Can I trust He won't lead me into another dangerous situation?"

"Jesus, can I trust You to keep me safe?"

Kim repeated the prayer. "Yes."

"Good. Would you like Jesus to bring His Father into the situation?"

Opening her eyes, Kim shook her head, "No. I think I've had enough for today."

"Are you sure? We can see what Father God thinks about your situation?"

"I'll be fine."

"That is completely okay. But when you decide to continue, find me or one of the team members, and we will be happy to pray with you."

"Thank you," Kim said. She dried the rest of her tears and shuffled away.

In this quick, on-the-spot, Sozo-type prayer, Kim's discomfort toward Father God prevented her from continuing. Had she elected to progress, Carol may have found some deep emotional wounds surrounding Kim's relationship with her earthly father that, once healed, would have given her the peace she needed in this season. Had they continued, Kim could have resolved these wounds and become more comfortable with the concept of encountering Father God. Instead of continuing, Kim decided to walk away. Sometimes people need time to process.

For Kim, Jesus's truths illuminated some important revelations. For Jim, the breakthrough was even more pronounced. As he allowed God's love to intervene, he fell to the floor a broken man and stood an adopted son. Although Kim received key insights into her situation, it would take more time for her to receive the wholeness that Jim experienced through his breakthrough with the Father.

To best understand the formation of orphan mindsets, we must analyze their origins. Like most beliefs, presuppositions, and convictions, orphan mindsets usually develop in childhood. Growing up, children learn to interpret life according to the messages communicated within their home. Children who suffer abuse, like Jim, usually grow up believing the world is unsafe. Having no protectors, they are forced to care for themselves.

Interpretations formed in our youth affect other relationships. Perceptions of God and others are skewed according to the way an individual experiences life. To rationalize pain and trauma, we can create false representations of reality. While such interpretations seem accurate to those who create them, a person's preconceptions skew meaning and lead to an ungodly outlook. In Sozo, we call this *seeing life through colored lenses.*

Even mature Christians can be deceived if viewing life through tinted glass. One who has a victim lens may interpret acts of kindness as manipulative or demeaning. Jim's colored lenses included a belief that God was scary. Without removing this perception, it was impossible for him to see God as safe. No amount of teaching could penetrate this suspicion. But when the lens was exposed and the truth revealed, Jim could see the truth of Father God's heart.

Most people suffer from multiple sets of colored lenses. These can have any number of labels such as *fear, rejection, pride, superiority, bullying,* or *jealousy.* Whichever of these lenses we identify, we work with Jesus to exchange those views for Christ's mindset:

> *We destroy arguments and every lofty opinion raised against the knowledge of God, and take every thought captive to obey Christ, being ready to punish every disobedience, when your obedience is complete* (2 Corinthians 10:5-6).

By taking each thought captive, we can come into agreement with Christ's mindset.

It has been said that every good story has three distinct characters: the *victim (one who feels threatened),* the *villain (one who is threatening),* and the *hero (one who, no matter what, understands he is powerful and has no need to be a threat or be threatened).* Victims see reality as unsafe. Partnering with a defeated mindset, they blame issues on others and either give up or wait for heroes to fix their mistakes. Villains see life as vulnerable to manipulation. They exploit others to achieve their goals. As Stephen De Silva points out in his Prosperous Soul teachings, both victims and villains partner (though at opposite ends) with an orphan spirit.

Heroes, however, see life through Christ's victorious mindset. Embracing what Christ accomplished at the cross, heroes realize they have already won. Unwilling to settle for anything less than God's promises, heroes win without intentionally hurting others.

When a client comes for a Sozo wearing a victim or villain lens, the "truth" he or she has brought into the situation opposes God's. Victims feel God is either too busy or unconcerned to intervene, but villains deny the possibility of even needing help. Both are powerful, deceptive lenses. Typically, the victim mindset goes hand in hand with self-pity, whereas villain mindsets walk with a spirit of justification.

Breaking a client free of a victim or villain mindset means introducing him or her to the One who knows truth. Difficult questions can be raised in a Sozo session, such as "Why does God let bad things happen?" Sozo ministers refuse to provide answers best left to God. Instead, they facilitate conversations between clients and the Lord. In such scenarios, colored lenses are exposed and replaced with God's truth.

Here is an example of a situation in which colored lenses were removed:

One afternoon, Teresa's client, Sue, made an appointment to develop a stronger connection with God.

Teresa asked, "How do you perceive Father God?"

"What do you mean?"

"How do you see Him?"

"He always seems distant. Every time I try to get close, all I feel is cold and empty."

"Repeat after me: 'I forgive my earthly father for being distant, for not wanting to be near me, and for not creating a space for me to feel safe or accepted. I renounce the lie that Father God does not want me close and does not have a safe place for me.'"

Sue repeated the prayer. Her eyes began to glisten.

"Father God, what is the truth?"

Sue's lips creased into an uncomfortable frown.

"What did God say?"

"How do I know it's Him? What if I'm making this stuff up?"

"Repeat after me: 'I forgive my earthly father for making me feel like anything I say is incorrect. I forgive him for making me feel like I have to weigh my words before I can speak them.'"

Sue repeated the prayer. Her face relaxed.

"I can't believe it. I was always afraid of not having the right answer for my dad's questions."

"What did Father God share with you earlier?"

"What if He was not serious about it?"

"Repeat after me: 'I forgive my earthly father for making fun of me when I was gullible.'"

At this, Sue began to weep. "That is how I feel most of the time. Like I'm a joke. That people are laughing at me."

"Would you like to forgive them, Sue?"

"I forgive everyone who made fun of me. I renounce the lie that Father God thinks of me as a joke. God, what's the truth? How do You see me?"

"Can you see, hear, or sense anything?"

Through tears, Sue responded, "His arms are open. And He has a big smile."

"What do you want to do?"

"Run into His arms. But what happens if He changes His mind?"

"Repeat after me: 'I forgive everyone in my life that would give me hope and then change their minds. I renounce the lie that Father God will also change His mind to love me. Father God, what is the truth?'"

"He says I'm powerful."

"Do you believe Him?"

Looking up, she responded with surprise, "Yes. I believe I actually do believe Him, and honestly I do feel more empowered."

"I break agreement with the lie that Father God is distant and is waiting to make fun of me. I tell rejection and fear to go, in Jesus's name."

Sue's smile widened.

"Do you still feel empty inside?"

"No."

"Ask God if you can run into His arms any time you'd like."

"He said yes, I can join Him whenever I want."

"Great."

God's intervention led to the removal of several of Sue's colored lenses. First, she believed God was distant. Teresa helped remove the lie by imparting forgiveness to Sue's earthly father. Second, Sue partnered with a fear of rejection. As with the previous lie, forgiving those who had reinforced this negativity brought her freedom.

Both lenses affected Sue's ability to see God's truth. With these lenses in place, Sue exhausted herself trying to rationalize her false perception of God's love. Thankfully, God replaced Sue's lenses with new truth. Doing so displaced her negative thoughts and strengthened her relationship with God.

The following chapters of this Sozo book are designed to help you remove colored lenses, heal the harm you carry from life, and connect you powerfully with God.

| Group Discussion Questions |

1. Can you perceive any ungodly mindsets you already know you battle?

2. If you don't already know of any ungodly mindset you are carrying, then ask God to reveal to you if you are wearing any "colored lenses" and record what He shows you.

| Activation |

1. With the ungodly mindset you have been carrying in mind, ask Father God where you first learned to believe this as truth.

2. Ask Him to show you where He was in the memory or event as He reveals it to you.

3. Ask God to reveal to you the truth of the situation.

4. Release forgiveness to those who harmed you in this incident.

5. Renounce the lies and/or mindsets you partnered with because of this event.

6. Hand God the "colored lenses" you have been wearing and viewing life through.

7. Ask God what He wants to give you in exchange for these lies/mindsets.

| Suggested Materials |

De Silva, Dawna. *Who's Your Daddy?* CD/DVD.

Frost, Jack. *Experiencing Father's Embrace.* Shippensburg, PA: Destiny Image, 2002. Print.

Liebscher, Teresa. *Bubble with Father God.* CD.

Liebscher, Teresa. *Father God's Shield.* CD.

Manwaring, Paul. *Kisses from a Good God: A Journey Through Cancer.* Shippensburg, PA: Destiny Image, 2012. Print. CD/DVD.

Chapter 4

GOD THE PROVIDER AND PROTECTOR

Grace, a mother in her 30s, entered Sarah's office. As they talked, Sarah discovered past abuses in Grace's relationship with her father. These, along with other wounds caused in childhood, created a strong sense of lack in the areas of provision and security.

Grace was now married, and although she and her husband had enough money to live comfortably, Grace could not shake her fear of poverty. She criticized her husband's spending and rarely bought things they needed—like healthier food, new tires for the car, and warm clothes for the kids. This reached a breaking point when her children caught colds because they lacked adequate clothing. After an intense argument with her husband, Grace decided to make an appointment.

"I don't know what's wrong with me," Grace said. "Every time I open my checkbook, I feel anxious."

"Why do you think that is?" Sarah asked.

"I don't know."

"Well," Sarah said, "why don't we bring this issue to Father God? Let's see what He thinks. Close your eyes."

Grace closed her eyes. Sarah led her through a simple prayer and recited each word carefully to allow her to repeat each one.

"Father God," Sarah said. "Are there any lies I am believing about myself?"

She allowed Grace a moment of silence. (In Sozo sessions, it is important not to interrupt discussions between a client and God.) After a minute of silence, Sarah asked if she heard, sensed, or saw anything.

"I saw clouds," Grace said. "And lightning."

"How did that make you feel?"

"Not very safe."

"Are you okay if we ask Father God another question?"

"Sure."

"Repeat after me: 'Father God, are there any lies I am believing about You?'"

Sarah gave Grace a full minute to process. After sensing she was ready, Sarah asked if Grace could hear, see, or sense anything.

"Yes," Grace said. "I heard that I believe God is unsafe."

"Where do you think you learned this lie?"

Grace froze. Sarah reminded her that this was a safe environment, that nothing she said would leave the room, and that freedom must be seized through risk. Grace raised her tear-stained face.

"I learned this lie from my father. Every Saturday, if I failed to do the chores, he would remove his belt and beat me. My mother would just stand there and watch. He never hit my brother. I made sure always to take the blame."

Confessing this weight, she buried her face in her palms and wept. Sarah gave her a moment to grieve. Feeling she was ready to continue, Sarah asked the next question.

"Would you like to bring this memory to Father God and see what He thinks?"

"Do you think it will help?"

"I know it will. Father God, would You show me where You were in this memory?"

Sarah asked Grace to repeat the prayer. Through expressions in Grace's face, Sarah could tell something important was happening. Sensing Grace was ready, Sarah asked what she could see, hear, or sense.

Wiping away tears, Grace recounted her vision with the Lord.

"I saw the Lord standing between me and my father. Every time he hit me, Father God took the worst of the blows. When the beating finished, God held me and said I was His precious daughter."

Before she could finish the sentence, tears filled Grace's eyes. She dabbed her face with a napkin and reclined in her seat. Eager to hear the encounter's effect, Sarah asked how she felt.

"Better," she said. "Being loved feels great."

"Good," Sarah said. "Let's thank Father God for His protection and see if there is anything else we need to address. Is that okay with you?"

"That sounds great."

"Repeat after me: 'Father God, thank You for revealing Your heart of protection. I receive the truth that You protected me in my moment of crisis—even when I felt alone. I receive Your truth that I am worthy of Your love and protection. I accept this truth in Jesus's name.'"

Before continuing with Grace, it is important to point out why Sarah used the word *protect* multiple times. Many of the issues addressed in the previous section stemmed from her memory of not feeling protected. Not getting this need met in childhood caused anxiety to follow her into adulthood. Grace needed to discover what lie(s) she believed about herself, others, and/or God and then confront those lies with God's truth. Only then could Heaven's reality of what happened (how God saw things) be released into her life.

Another reason Sarah used the word *protect* is that according to a tool presented in Sozo seminars called the Father Ladder, three key needs are met through the Father—*provision*, *protection*, and *identity*. This tool will be looked at in-depth in the following chapter. In Grace's painful memory, her need to feel protected was violated by her father's harsh discipline. Experiences like these, where fathers not only fail to protect their children but harm them as well, create the perfect environment in which lies can grow.

In Grace's situation, Holy Spirit prompted her to renounce the lie that she was unworthy of her father's love. This, then, confronted the lie that Grace was unworthy of Father God's protection. Although Grace never voiced this thought, partnering with the Holy Spirit prodded Sarah to include this in the prayer. It turned out to be exactly what Grace needed to hear. By addressing the wounds left by her dad, Grace finally recognized her unmet need, brought it to God, and received healing.

A great deal of what goes on in a Sozo session relies on partnership with the Holy Spirit. Sarah's inclination to include the word "protect" over and over was the Lord's idea. This is where partnering with God comes into full effect. In Sozo, the importance of relying on God's Spirit is constantly stressed.

In truth, none of us can really do anything for a person who makes a Sozo appointment. All we can do, and what Sozo team members are taught to offer the client, is to partner with God to work through issues together. Sozo ministers trust God to reveal the issues needing healing at the proper time. In this way, it keeps pressure off the ministers to perform and gives glory to God.

Sarah allowed Grace time to process. The pain of years of abuse, stimulated by the lie that she was unworthy of protection, dwindled. Slowly, she relaxed. Feeling ready to progress, Sarah asked if Grace was ready.

"Yes."

"All right. Picture Father God. What do you see?"

This time Grace seemed comfortable. Sarah could see a smile sneaking onto her client's lips. After a brief period of silence, Sarah asked if Grace could see, hear, or sense anything.

"Yes. I see Father God. He and I are walking in a garden, talking about each other's favorite plants."

"How does that make you feel?"

"Happy. I don't think I've ever interacted with God outside of church."

"Do you mind if we ask God another question?"

"Not at all."

"Repeat after me: 'Father God, are there any other lies I am believing about myself or You that we need to deal with?'"

Again, Sarah gave Grace a minute to search.

"God said I'm believing the lie that because of my dad's abuse, I'm damaged goods."

"What does God think of that?"

Grace smiled. "He said I am His princess. He said nothing the enemy throws at me will succeed."

"How does that make you feel?"

"Relieved. But it feels too good to be true."

"Well, then, let's do some forgiving. Repeat after me: 'Father God, I choose to forgive my earthly father for teaching me the lie that I am damaged goods. I renounce the lie that I have to partner with his or anyone's negative actions. I hand to You the judgment I have made about myself that I am damaged goods. Thank You that I am Your daughter and a beautiful princess, that You have called me Your own and have established me for Your plans. I receive this truth in Jesus's name.'" (See Second Timothy 1:9.)

After repeating the prayer, Sarah gave Grace a full minute to soak in these truths. After Sarah felt that Grace was ready to continue, she asked Grace how she felt. Opening her eyes, Grace smiled.

"I believe it now."

"Great," Sarah said. "Let's see what else Father God has to say about you."

"Wonderful."

In this section of our Sozo session, identity was the focus. After showing Grace that she was worthy of being protected, God was about to tell her the reason why. This is typical for victims of abuse who have difficulty believing God's truth. It seems so out of reach. When this happens, prayers of forgiveness work to release bitterness and invite healing. (See Matthew 6:14-15.)

In Grace's example, the person she needed to forgive was her father. Because of her unsafe relationship with her dad, proper identity was never spoken over her. This is a responsibility all parents are given to offer to their children—especially fathers. Mothers contribute identity as well; however, we have found that dads tend to be a child's primary source of identity. We have seen that when children fail in school, complete a task inaccurately, or even strike out in their time at bat, what their dads say to them tends to skew their view of their identity more profoundly than what their mothers or friends say about them.

If a father criticizes or punishes a child for mistakes made, then a colored lens of punishment can easily be added to the way the child will view life and, ultimately, Father God. These children tend to grow up with a fear of failure and/or a need to perform perfectly. If a father says everything is fine and sends the child back out to play, then the child will see mistakes as a process toward completion rather than something to fear. The latter example is a wonderful representation of our Father God, who constantly forgives our sins, picks us up from where we have fallen, and encourages us to continue on our journey.

Unfortunately, Grace never received this affirmation from her father. Because of this, her identity spoke of her as damaged goods rather than someone to be valued. Only by encountering the Heavenly Father and hearing His affirmation could she receive healing of these wounds and believe in herself.

Because Grace worked through issues of protection in the first example, she could picture Father God as loving and caring. In Sozo sessions, it is always important to discover how clients perceive or see the Father. If the image is scary, we work with the person to discover what lies he or she is believing. If the client is having difficulty hearing from the Father, we turn to either Jesus or the Holy Spirit as a direct line of communication.

This often works for people who grew up with religious, legalistic backgrounds. Such folks grew up being taught that one cannot hear, see, or sense God. In their minds, to do so is blasphemy. In these instances, it is best to work on issues with the Father through whichever member of the Godhead the client is most comfortable with. This allows the person to build a connection to God gradually, uncovering lies that may have otherwise remained hidden.

In most sessions, ministers begin by asking clients which of the three members of the Godhead they are most comfortable with. This allows a trust to be built between the client and the Sozo minister, creating a safe atmosphere. However, Sozo guidelines are principles, not rules. It is important to allow the Spirit freedom to lead. If the Sozo minister does not feel the need to open a Sozo session in this way, that is fine. It is always best to follow the Spirit.

In Grace's situation, the most comfortable entry would have been through Jesus or the Holy Spirit. However, feeling Holy Spirit's promptings toward the Father, Sarah introduced Father God first. Fortunately for Grace, the prompting succeeded. Grace's hunger for the Father's love overshadowed her fears.

Sometimes, this is not the case. A person's fears may keep him or her from wanting to address a member of the Godhead. Take Jim, for instance, from the previous chapter. Because of his abusive relationship with his father, Jim was not willing to approach the concept of a loving God. Remember how even praying to the Heavenly Father caused anxiety? This is because he viewed God through a victim mentality rather than as a son. Note in Jim's instance, Dawna asked Jesus to take him to His Father. After he worked through several lies and discarded colored lenses, he grasped the concept that not all fathers, especially not the Heavenly Father, are like his.

It is important to note how Grace's situation built upon multiple precepts. Before asking her to hear truth from Father God, Sarah asked Grace to picture Him. Sarah then asked Grace to discover what lies she believed about the Father before moving on into deeper relationship with Him. This is one goal of Sozo—to identify and disempower lies. If Grace was unable to even picture God as safe and protecting, how could she expect to hear something safe and truthful? Our eyes see what they expect to see. By correcting Grace's colored lenses, God's true love could be revealed.

Grace sat and pondered the words. Moments before, Sarah had asked if there was anything else she wanted to work through in this session. She looked to Sarah with hope in her eyes.

"The reason I came here is because of my issues with money. My husband says I hoard everything. My poor kids...it's just so hard growing up with nothing. I don't want them to go through what I did."

"I understand. You want what's best for your children. Why don't we..."

"See what Father God has to say?" Grace said.

"Exactly. Repeat after me: 'Father God, are there any lies I am believing about my finances?'"

After this, Grace paused. After about 15 seconds, she lifted her face.

"He said I am believing the lie that my finances will run out. That I will never have enough."

"Ask Father God where you first learned this lie."

"From my dad. He drank often and hardly had any money for us kids. I know it's not the biggest deal, but it was always hard to go back to school after Christmas and hear what all the other kids got. My brother and I didn't even have warm clothes."

"I see. Do you see this pattern developing in your own life?"

"Yes."

"Would you like to forgive your father and deal with this issue of provision?"

"Yes."

"Great. Repeat after me: 'Father God, I choose to forgive my dad for teaching me the lie that there will never be enough, that I will always be hungry. I ask You, Father God, to forgive me for believing this lie and hoarding money to try to protect my children. I hand this lie to You, Father, and renounce ties to any bitterness in my heart. What truth do You have for me in exchange?'"

After Grace finished repeating the prayer, Sarah gave her a full minute to process. Once finished, Grace sat up in her seat.

"God gave me a huge money bag—one that was almost as big as the earth. He said this was His source of income and promised I would never run out. He said I could access it whenever I want."

"That's great. How does that make you feel?"

"Pretty good."

"Did He say anything about your tendency to hoard things?"

"No. He didn't need to. I realize how silly that is. The first thing I will do after this session is go buy my kids some decent clothes."

"I'm sure they will love it. Now is there anything else you think God wants to work on?"

Grace bowed her head. After a few minutes, Sarah asked her what she could see, hear, or sense. After a minute, Grace shook her head. "No."

"All right. How do you feel?"

"Pretty good."

"What are you going to do to walk these truths out?"

"Pray. And keep working on the truths God showed me in this session."

"That's wise. If, for any reason, some of these truths seem to weaken in the coming weeks, know that is a common tactic of the enemy to discourage breakthrough. Sometimes after gaining ground there is a possibility to lose spoil. The goal is not to lose heart and to keep continuing forward. That way, your progress will continue."

Sarah handed her a piece of paper.

"On this paper, I wrote down all of Father God's truths. You won't see any lies or negative areas we worked through. Post this on your fridge or beside your bed—anywhere it is easy to find. It will remind you of God's truth in times of difficulty. Read through it, ask God to expand the truths you learned here today, and ask the Holy Spirit to point out to you Scriptures that correspond to these truths."

Grace took the paper. "Thank you."

"You're welcome. I expect to hear good things about you in the coming months."

"I can't wait to give you an update."

"I can't wait to hear it."

"Thank you."

Grace took her piece of paper, stood, and exited a different person—someone with access to the Father. Her journey into a deeper experience with God was underway. Her connection to the Father would allow her to hear His voice more clearly speaking over her, thereby strengthening their relationship. More work would be needed. This encounter was not meant to fix all of her life's problems. She would need to continue developing connections to Jesus and Holy Spirit in order to root out all the mindsets that had been implanted. In time, these connections would come. For now, she was enjoying a fresh relationship with the Father.

In this last section, Grace experienced breakthrough in her need for *provision*. After forgiving her father for a lack of financial stability, Grace experienced healing. In this Sozo session, all three needs (*provision*, *protection*, and *identity*) required God's truth.

Not all Sozo sessions require such depth with the Father. A person may have an excellent sense of identity, yet a complete dysfunction in the realm of finances. Someone may believe she is worthy of protection but have no grid for how God sees her. Whatever the client's needs, the Sozo minister's duty is to partner with God to bring those needs to Him, expose any wounds, dispel demonic attachments, and facilitate an exchange of those lies for God's truth.

Like so many others, Grace was taking the first steps needed to begin a life of intimate connection with God. She left believing the truths of God's Word: that God was for her, not against her (see Rom. 8:31); that He was Jehovah-Jireh, "the God who provides" (see Gen. 22:14); and that she had access to Him without fear of punishment (see Heb. 4:16). She walked through the door with Jesus to enter God's presence without fear of Him and was able to begin building a healthy connection with the Father. She would now be able to begin to trust Father God to meet her emotional, physical, and spiritual needs of protection, provision, and identity. New dimensions were going to begin opening up in her life.

When a client receives such paradigm shifts, we usually ask her to walk out these newly found truths and rebook a Sozo in the following three to six months. From there, the minister should make sure the client has retained the truths revealed in the prior Sozo and build on them to ferret out any other lies or ungodly paradigms to which she might have been listening and reacting.

| Group Discussion Questions |

1. Are there any lies you are believing about provision?

2. Are you worried about your finances?

3. Do you find yourself hoarding resources?

4. Do you have a hard time not overspending or keeping to a budget?

5. Do you find yourself consistently buying less or more than you actually need?

6. Are there any lies you are believing about God's protection or lack thereof?

7. Do you think of yourself as a fearful person?

8. Do you worry about what other people think of you?

9. Do you wish God had made you a braver person?

10. Are there any lies you are believing about yourself?

11. Do you often compare yourself to others?

12. Do you ever find yourself jealous of other people's gifts or lives?

13. Do you consider yourself not very good-looking?

14. Do you feel like you are disqualified from receiving as much from God as others get to receive?

15. Are you ashamed of your past?

16. Are there things from which you cannot seem to get free?

| Activation |

For each question to which you answered "yes," walk through this prayer:

1. Close your eyes and ask Father God where you learned these habits, fears, lies, or mindsets.

2. Ask Him to show you where He was when these habits, fears, lies, or mindsets were formed.

3. Ask Him to reveal His truth to you about the situation He shows you.

4. Release forgiveness to anyone who harmed you or taught you these lies, fears, or mindsets.

5. Hand to Him any ungodly mindsets formed in you or lies you believed from these experiences.

6. Renounce participation and agreements with any demonic attachments and/or vows you made because of these situations.

7. Ask Father God what He wants to give you in exchange for what you have renounced and handed to Him.

8. Thank Him for His truth and the freedom you received because of His truth.

| Suggested Materials |

De Silva, Stephen. *Money and the Prosperous Soul: Tipping the Scales of Favor and Blessing.* Grand Rapids, MI: Chosen Books, 2010. Print.

De Silva, Stephen. *Prosperous Soul Foundations.* CD/DVD/Manual.

Johnson, Bill. *Generosity: A Military Move.* CD/DVD.

Chapter 5

THE FATHER LADDER UNVEILED

We can begin our discussion of the Father Ladder with a brief overview:

In summary, the Father Ladder is a tool that the Sozo Ministry uses to help clarify the connections between lies that have been learned from childhood and the relationships we have formed with each member of the Godhead. For example, a person who experienced a difficult relationship with his earthly father may have difficulty experiencing a safe relationship with Father God. We have found that our relationship with the members of the Godhead often corresponds to what we believe is true about our early family experiences. Therefore, if we are convinced fathers are unsafe or scary, accepting the concept of a loving "Father" God will be difficult.

Where does the concept of the Father Ladder originate? It was first introduced to us by a pastor friend, Alan Ray, as he taught us about the needs and fears that he found with his clients while counseling. As he discussed the needs we have as humans and how God designed us to get these needs met by Him, we saw that what we were encountering in Sozo sessions lined up consistently with this idea. This tool borrows heavily from Scripture's description of the institution of the human family. The first institution God created was the family. This unit represents the function of each member of the Godhead—Father God, Jesus, and Holy Spirit (see Gen. 1:26). When family members fail to fulfill their roles, the resulting pain and confusion can easily transfer to our understanding of God, Jesus, and Holy Spirit.

The Father Ladder chart displays our needs corresponding to our being: body, soul, and spirit. Each component has specific needs:

- The body has the need for identity/value, protection, and provision (see Job 42:10).

- The soul needs communication and companionship (see 1 Pet. 3:20).

- The spirit needs comfort and teaching (see Rom. 8:16).

Here is a chart to help you visualize this principle:

	BODY: Identity/value Protection Provision	
	SOUL: Companionship Communication	
	SPIRIT: Comfort Teaching	

The middle section of the Father Ladder shows each need as it connects specifically to spirit, soul, and body. We believe that these needs were placed in us by God and exist from conception to death. Based on a person's relationship with his or her family, he or she will have a perception as to whether these needs will either be met or ignored, thus forming mindsets as a child that carry over into adulthood.

When family members do not meet the needs of their children, spouses, or friends, lies develop. These lies can make it difficult for individuals to connect with other people, themselves, and God. The Father Ladder helps ministers gain information about these lies quickly and works to break the associated beliefs we attributed to the Godhead.

Contrary to what some world agendas are trying to tell us today, the family unit has three distinct parts: a father, a mother, and siblings (unless you are an only child). We have found that each part has a role in aiding the development of healthy individuals.

	BODY: Identity/value Protection Provision	**FATHER**
	SOUL: Companionship Communication	**SIBLINGS/ FRIENDS**
	SPIRIT: Comfort Teaching	**MOTHER**

We have seen that children establish their identity primarily from the way their father communicates with them. How a father relates to his children and what he says to and about them will often translate into how they view themselves and how they interact with others. When Father God says at Jesus's baptism, "This is My beloved Son in whom I am well pleased," He is clearly imparting the identity and authority of Jesus (see Matt. 3:17; 17:5; Mark 1:11; Luke 3:22). Jesus's confidence in His relationship with Father God cannot be understated (see John 5:19).

When a father fails to let his children know how he sees them and who they are through his eyes, identities can become confused. This confusion can lead to serious dysfunctions in behavior as children then test boundaries and worldly options in an attempt to establish who they truly are. Children who are confident in who they are tend to act accordingly. The child's inner belief system, formed by his earthly father's opinions, positions him for healthy, successful life choices.

Fathers also have the responsibility to provide protection. In a healthy family, when children feel frightened, they look to their father for safety. He is the one to whom they run because usually he is seen as the bigger and stronger person in the family. Repeatedly, we have seen how adults have difficulty feeling safe when, as children, their fathers failed to provide protection, or worse, contributed to an unsafe environment.

Lastly, the father is normally considered to be the provider of financial security within the family even if the mother has the ability to earn more income. When a father fails to provide for the family, children tend to create mindsets of lack that carry over into their adulthood.

In the family unit, it is siblings and/or friends who generally meet the needs of communication and companionship. They are the ones with whom we talk and divulge our secrets. Even when children have a good relationship with their parents, their deepest secrets usually are shared only with their friends. Squabbling between friends and sib-lings is a major way by which children learn boundaries and conflict resolution. Through social interactions, we learn how far we can push ourselves on others, how much we can take from others, and where to set and recognize healthy boundaries between these two extremes. When bullying occurs with siblings and friends, harmful mindsets can be created and judgments made about future adult relationships.

The earthly mother is the one most responsible for the comfort and instruction of her children. Mothers suckle their offspring; they are equipped to bring nutrients and provide comfort. Mothers, not fathers, are equipped to nourish their babies. In a healthy family, this early connection between newborn and mother becomes a time of bonding that paves the way for an ability to receive and give nurture later in life. In nearly every culture, the mother is given the job of raising the newborn through infancy until the child is able to care for itself.

We have found that if a mom is controlling and continually cor-rects the child's mistakes, the child learns the lie that he or she has to be perfect to please others. Conversely, if the mother never corrects her child, the child grows up having to set his or her own boundaries. This often leads to a sense of fear of failure or an unhealthy degree of self-sufficiency.

Father God, Jesus, and the Holy Spirit (the Trinity) represent the three aspects of the Godhead. Applying this to the Father Ladder, we see that each member of the Godhead can be distinctly connected to the needs of body, soul, and spirit. Just as each member of the family has a function in meeting the needs of our being, each member of the Godhead tends to meet corresponding needs. We should note here that father and mother figures can also represent to us a good or bad view of Father God and Holy Spirit.

Our perspectives of each family member can have a great effect on how we do or do not connect with the Godhead. Here is a grid to illustrate this concept:

	BODY: Identity/value Protection Provision	FATHER Male teachers/ pastors Male scout lead- ers/coaches Grandfathers Uncles
FATHER GOD		
JESUS	SOUL: Companionship Communication	SIBLINGS/ FRIENDS
HOLY SPIRIT	SPIRIT: Comfort Teaching	MOTHER Female teachers/ pastors Female coaches/ activity leaders Grandmothers Aunts

In Sozo after Sozo, we have found that clients have trouble understanding their identities in the Lord if their fathers did not help them develop this as a child. Because they have difficulty understanding their value, they have difficulty knowing what Father God thinks about them.

When earthly fathers are not present to protect or provide, children tend to fear the lack of provision. Out of this fear, many transfer feelings of abandonment and isolation onto Father God. This mindset can cause us to filter His truth of protection and provision through these ungodly lenses.

To help with these issues, Sozo works to provide a way for the client to encounter Father God in order to experience His truths of protection, provision, and identity.

The Bible says that Jesus is our companion and best friend. Thus, we have found that our interactions with our siblings and friends often mirror how we believe Jesus interacts with us. An older sibling who was, for example, forced to parent the younger sibling may believe Jesus wants to force him to take excess responsibility. This may cause him to fear he will have to partner with a ministry or career he does not wish to do. He may also believe Jesus will give him a destiny he is incapable of carrying out.

A younger sibling may think an older sibling will try to control her. Believing this, she may formulate a lie that Jesus, too, wants to control her—that He is not out for her best but to make things better for Himself or others.

Friendship can be an area where people feel devalued. Friends are supposed to understand and include us. If this does not happen, we may tend to believe that even Jesus does not want to include us. How many times have you heard Christians say, "Yeah, I know He loves me, but I'm not really sure He likes me." If we carry this belief into our service with the Lord, we will forever be striving to get His approval rather than resting in His acceptance and grace.

To heal these areas, Sozo ministers work at initiating a conversation with Jesus. Freedom comes to clients when they experience the truth of His unconditional acceptance, communication, and companionship.

We have found that when a mother is absent from her children's lives through their early years, either physically or emotionally, they are often confused whether or not they can expect to have their needs met. They can easily transfer these feelings onto their understanding of the Holy Spirit. If the mother is not physically or emotionally available, the father can and needs to take over this responsibility. However, we have found that this can confuse normal parental roles and can affect our adult relationships with God and the Holy Spirit.

If a mother tries to control her children through guilt and manipulation, they can construct a wall that guards against the promptings of the Holy Spirit. We find that most Christians who keep a "safe" distance between themselves and the Holy Spirit have what we call in Sozo a "mother wound."

To heal these issues, the Sozo minister encourages clients to forgive their mother and to connect themselves to a loving, caring, and powerful Holy Spirit.

When using the Father Ladder, Sozo ministers typically follow these steps:

1. Get information.

2. Ask the individual how he or she views, senses, or pictures Father God, Jesus, and Holy Spirit (one at a time).

3. Ask the client what he or she believes about God, Jesus, or the Holy Spirit (one at a time).

4. Have the client forgive whichever family member corresponds with the Godhead member from whom he or she feels distant. Use information gained from step one.

5. Renounce: Have the client renounce the lie he or she believes about Father God, Jesus, or the Holy Spirit.

6. Ask for truth: After renouncing the lie, have the client ask Father God, Jesus, or the Holy Spirit for truth. Allow time for the client to interact with God. At times, receiving truth takes multiple "pray-throughs."

Here are some examples to show how Sozo ministers can use the Father Ladder:

If an individual senses Father God is cold or distant, have her forgive her earthly father for being physically and emotionally unavailable. Next, have the client renounce the lie that Father God will treat her the same way. Then ask Father God for the truth. Allow the client to hear for herself what He has to say.

If an individual feels that Jesus does not listen to his prayers, have him forgive the siblings and/or friends who did not value his company. After this, have the person renounce the lie that Jesus also does not value his company. Ask Jesus for the truth. As with Father God, allow the individual to hear what Christ has to say.

If an individual feels the Holy Spirit is unavailable, have her forgive her mother for being absent in her daily life. Have her renounce the lie that the Holy Spirit is distant. Lastly, allow the individual to hear what the Holy Spirit says.

(NOTE: It is important to realize that forgiveness may need to extend past the initial family members and incorporate some of the other people representing the parental examples shown in the final diagram of the Father Ladder.)

To better understand the process of using the Father Ladder, here is a practical example, which can be used for either Father God, Jesus, or the Holy Spirit:

Jenny, a Sozo minister, sat across from Nancy, a recent convert to Christianity. Wanting to discover any hindrances blocking her relationship with God, Nancy scheduled a Sozo session. She sat across from the Sozo minister happily, ready to dispel any hindrances.

Opening the session, Jenny asked, "How do you view Father God?"

Nancy furrowed her brow. "What do you mean?"

"How do you see Him?"

Getting the picture, Nancy began: "I know He loves me, but isn't that what He is supposed to do? Every time I try to communicate with Him, He feels distant. Maybe I've done something wrong?"

Identifying the lie, Jenny began, "Repeat after me: 'I forgive my earthly father for not allowing me to feel safe when talking with him. I forgive him for being distant and for not telling me how important I was to him—especially when I did something wrong.'"

Nancy repeated the prayer. Jenny allowed her to add her own words when necessary to express accurately her relationship to her father. When Nancy finished the prayer, Jenny continued.

"Repeat after me: 'I renounce the lie that Father God is distant. I renounce the lie that I'm not important enough for Father God to communicate with me.'"

Nancy repeated the prayer. Jenny allowed her time to process. When she sensed Nancy was ready, Jenny continued.

"Repeat after me: 'Father God, what's the truth?'"

After Nancy repeated the question, Jenny waited to see if she could hear or sense truth. Nodding, Nancy explained the fun pictures Father God displayed. As with any Sozo session, God's answers to her were unique and tailored to her needs.

(NOTE: Typically, if a client can hear or sense truth, the Sozo minister proceeds by asking if he or she believes what Father God said. If he does, healing occurs. If he does not receive truth or has difficulty believing it, there is another lie waiting to be found.)

In this short exercise, Nancy heard the Lord's truth and implemented it into her life. At times, however, an individual does not hear or accept the truth revealed. If this happens, it simply means there are more lies needing to be dealt with. This can be solved through further use of the Father Ladder in the session or other tools discussed later in this book.

| Group Discussion Questions |

Father God

1. How do you view, sense, or see Father God?

2. Ask Father God if there is a lie you are believing about Him.

3. Ask Him where you learned this lie.

4. Release forgiveness to anyone who taught you this lie as truth (this could be any male authority figure in your life).

5. Ask God what truth He wants to give you in exchange for this lie.

6. Allow this truth to settle in your spirit and ask Him to reveal to you a Scripture that depicts this truth.

7. Ask God what He thinks about you.

Jesus

1. How do you view, sense, or see Jesus?

2. Ask Him if there is a lie you are believing about Him.

3. Ask Him where you learned this lie.

4. Release forgiveness to anyone who taught you this lie as truth.

5. Ask Jesus what truth He wants to give you in exchange for this lie.

6. Allow this truth to settle in your spirit and ask Him to reveal to you a Scripture that depicts this truth.

7. Ask Jesus what He thinks about you.

Holy Spirit

1. How do you view, sense, or see the Holy Spirit?

2. Ask Holy Spirit if there is a lie you are believing about Him.

3. Ask Him where you learned this lie.

4. Release forgiveness to anyone who taught you this lie as truth (this could be any female authority figure in your life).

5. Ask Him what truth He wants to give you in exchange for this lie.

6. Allow this truth to settle in your spirit and ask Him to reveal to you a Scripture that depicts this truth.

7. Ask the Holy Spirit what He thinks about you.

| Suggested Materials |

De Silva, Dawna and Teresa Liebscher. *Sozo Basic*. CD/DVD/ Manual.

Chapter 6

HOLY SPIRIT AS TEACHER AND COMFORTER

Perhaps the least understood Person of the Trinity by many Christians is the Holy Spirit. Besides His scriptural appearances in the form of a dove (see Matt. 3:16), a gust of wind (see Acts 2:2), and tongues of fire (see Acts 2:3), no one actually knows what God's Spirit looks like. The word itself, "spirit," can denote a mysterious, intangible entity. Because of this uncertain physical quality, our understanding of the Holy Spirit may pale in comparison with Father God and Jesus.

Investigating God's Word, we see the Holy Spirit described as a teacher, empowerer, nurturer, and helper. Whether He is appearing concretely or abstractly, His role remains the same. In times of weakness, He strengthens. In times of sorrow, He comforts.

In Sozo, we teach that the Holy Spirit addresses the needs of *comfort*, *teaching*, and *nurturing*:

> *But the Comforter, which is the Holy Ghost, whom the Father will send in My name, He shall teach you all things, and bring all things to your remembrance, whatsoever I have said unto you* (John 14:26 KJV).

The Holy Spirit helps nurture our walk:

> *Likewise the Spirit helps us in our weakness. For we do not know what to pray for as we ought, but the Spirit Himself*

intercedes for us with groanings too deep for words (Romans 8:26).

The Holy Spirit interacts with our lives as both a teacher and a comforter. Seeing Him as our teacher, we learn to follow His promptings. Seeing Him as our nurturer, we take our pain to Him instead of trying to self-comfort with other worldly options.

In the Father Ladder diagram, the Holy Spirit represents relationship with our earthly mothers or other care-giving females from our formative years. The reason for this is that, most often, mothers act as the comforters, nurturers, and teachers in the family unit. For example, it is very natural for children who injure themselves to run to mom for comfort. Mothers are also the ones who get most of the two-year-olds' "why" questions.

It is important to note that these are not hard and fast rules. Mothers also provide protection, provision, and identity. Fathers likewise bring comfort and instruction. Sometimes older children take over protective roles for younger siblings. Each family member contributes to the overall health, wellness, and growth of a child. We have found that those who lacked a mother's teaching, comfort, or nurturing usually carry wounds that need to be healed. These areas often affect their relationship with the Holy Spirit. To live powerfully, we need to get these wounds healed that were created from a failed connection with our mothers and establish a strong connection with the Holy Spirit.

For example, children who received little to no comfort from their mothers growing up tend to carry an underlying sense of anxiety. Because they rarely experienced comfort, these children grow up not believing they are protected when taking risks. They learn that no one will be there to comfort them when they step out and fail. Individuals who struggle in this area tend to close themselves off and avoid risk.

To heal wounds created from detached, abusive, or manipulative mothers, Sozo ministers lead the client through identification, renunciation, repentance, and exchange. After identifying the lie(s), Sozo ministers have clients renounce their ties with them and exchange them for God's truth. Only then can they correctly connect with the Holy Spirit.

Rob experienced this process while engaged in a Sozo session.

Curious to know more about God's presence, Rob settled into his chair across from the Sozo minister. At first, he was hesitant. He had not grown up with a strong connection with the Holy Spirit. Interestingly enough, he also did not have a strong connection with his mother. Repulsed by physical touch, she had rarely ever interacted with him in a physical way. Rob's primary love language was touch. Obviously, this did not help their relationship. This breakdown in communication through physical touch meant that Rob never truly believed that his mother loved him.

In the session, the Sozo minister asked Rob to forgive his mother for not making it feel safe to allow physical touch between them. Rob repeated the prayer. Although his physical stance did not signal a major emotion, the minister could tell something deep was happening. After about only 30 seconds of processing, Rob looked at the minister and said that he thought all the disconnection between himself and his mother was his fault. The minister asked him to repeat a prayer of renunciation and wait for what the Holy Spirit had to say.

Rob repeated the prayer: "I renounce the lie that it is all my fault that there is a disconnect between my mother and me. I renounce the lie that Holy Spirit will treat me the same as my mother and that even though He is around at all times, He does not want to interact physically with me. Holy Spirit, what is the truth?"

After allowing Rob time to process, the minister asked, "What do you hear, sense, or see?"

Surprised, Rob responded that the Holy Spirit apologized for how his mother had treated him. In addition, Holy Spirit wanted him to know that he had permission to interact with His presence physically.

His curiosity piqued, Rob said yes. The second he spoke, the Lord's presence fell. Rob started to laugh. He asked if he could sit in Holy Spirit's lap. Holy Spirit said yes.

Rob's laughter began to build. The minister guessed why—the Holy Spirit was tickling him. After the Holy Spirit finished, the minister asked how Rob felt. Rob said he felt great. While the Holy Spirit was tickling him, Rob was being told about God's truths. He was no longer lost, broken, or abandoned. He had access to an eternal comforter, instructor, and nurturer. Afterward, the minister asked Rob if he believed what the Holy Spirit had said. Without delay, Rob said yes.

In this brief encounter, Rob developed a connection with the Holy Spirit. Areas in his life such as doubt, fear, and insecurity met their match with the presence of God's loving Spirit. Holy Spirit knew exactly what Rob needed to hear to receive blessing. Not having his love language met as a child, Rob never truly experienced his mother's love. She may have truly loved him, but the ways she displayed that love did not match how he needed to receive it.

The Holy Spirit's embracing of Rob helped establish his understanding of comfort and self-worth. Though this encounter would not have worked for everyone, the Lord, in His infinite wisdom, knew exactly what Rob needed. This is why Sozo sessions are unique, tailored to each individual. No two people have the same path to healing.

For another client, Lucas, the lack of connection to the Holy Spirit created anxiety in his relationship with the church. Meant to be a place of peace and interaction with the Lord, church, instead, presented a non-stop experience of fear and anxiety. The son of an inner healing and deliverance minister, Lucas had watched his parents, associate pastors, minister from the stage all his life. Now, at 16, he had just completed his prayer servant training and was asked to serve at the front. Today, he would be released to lay hands on the sick and see them made well. This is, at least, what Lucas expected.

The main issue was that Lucas did not have a personal, intimate relationship with the Holy Spirit. He had grown up in the church, seen miracles performed, and heard all about the mysteries of God. He could tell visitors about all the miracles that had happened in or outside his church. However, these miracles never came from his own hands, and he had not yet trained himself to hear from the Holy Spirit.

After the senior pastor closed his sermon and asked the prayer servants to come forward, Lucas followed his parents and fellow prayer servants to the front. When he reached the stage, the minister handed him the microphone and asked for a word of knowledge. Instantly, Lucas froze. He stared vacantly into the auditorium searching for an angel, a dove, or some tongue of fire—some sign from God. Seconds passed. Finally, Lucas handed the microphone to the pastor. He descended the steps and headed straight for the restroom.

Upon returning from his break, Lucas took his spot at the prayer line. As the first person approached him, he was struggling with inner doubt: *Do I have what it takes to pray for others? I hope I don't get someone to pray for who really needs a miracle.* When the person arrived in front of him, Lucas asked what the person needed prayer for. He answered, "Stage four cancer."

Lucas blushed. He looked to Heaven, asked God to be raptured, and began praying. The gentleman left content and full of peace but, as far as he knew, still carrying cancer. Lucas left discouraged and disappointed that God had not "shown up" for the man as he prayed.

This situation occurs when we lack an intimate relationship with the Holy Spirit. If we have not cultivated a relationship with the

"Comforter," how can we expect to comfort others? If we have not experienced the "Counselor," how can we be confident to counsel others?

Lucas blamed himself for the lack of instant evidence of healing. Because of his self-talk of ridicule, punishment, and self-doubt, he scheduled a Sozo appointment. A lie was getting in the way of his peace. Lucas did not know it yet, but he was about to be set free.

Lucas sat in his session and described the recent events that brought him in.

The Sozo minister waited until Lucas finished and opened with a simple question: "Would you like to invite the Holy Spirit and see what He thinks of the situation?"

Lucas nodded.

"Close your eyes and repeat after me: 'Holy Spirit, are there any lies I'm believing about You?'"

Lucas repeated the prayer. The Sozo minister allowed him time to process.

"Did you hear, see, or sense anything?"

"I don't think so. I don't see how I could believe anything false about the Spirit."

"Okay, let's try this. Repeat after me: 'Holy Spirit, are there any lies I'm believing about myself?'"

Lucas shifted in his seat.

"He said I'm believing the lie that I'm not worthy to be used. And I don't feel like He'll step out and help me when I take risks."

"Ask the Holy Spirit where you learned this lie."

Lucas mumbled a silent prayer. He lifted his face.

"My mother."

"Repeat after me: 'I forgive my mother for not celebrating in my failures when I took risks and for not giving me permission to fail when I tried my best. I renounce the lie that You, Holy Spirit, are disappointed and will not use me when I step out in faith. Holy Spirit, what's the truth?'"

Lucas repeated the prayer.

"What do you hear, sense, or see?"

Lucas opened his eyes.

"Holy Spirit is laughing. He's shaking off the lies that I was believing. He is showing me a trampoline He has set out for the times I need to jump out and take risks. He is telling me that the morning at church when I was scanning the auditorium for help, He was there giving me a word, but I was too scattered to see it. I can't believe I didn't notice it."

"Repeat after me: 'Thank You, Holy Spirit, for providing me with a word for the person who came up to me for prayer. I ask You to train my ears and eyes to hear and see Your voice. I renounce the lie that You are disappointed in me for not catching Your word. Thank You that You give us second chances and that this did not disqualify me from being used by You in the future. I ask for the courage, Holy Spirit, to take risks with You. Thank You for showing me that this man's lack of immediate breakthrough has nothing to do with how well You work through me. Holy Spirit, what truth do You want me to know?'"

Lucas repeated the prayer. He craned his ears to listen.

"What's He saying?"

Lucas grinned. "Holy Spirit's saying that He can't wait for my adventures. I have to seize them and charge on ahead."

"How does that make you feel?"

"Empowered."

"Repeat after me: 'Thank You, Holy Spirit, for blessing me with risk. I renounce all ties to fear and anxiety. I receive blessing, truth, and the power of Your anointing. I give myself permission to step out and pray for others in Jesus's name. I repent for partnering with fear, perfectionism, and performance, and I hand to You, Jesus, all ties to the demonic realm that I have allowed in partnering with these lies. I command fear, self-doubt, performance, perfectionism, and shame to leave me now in Your Holy name.'"

Lucas finished the prayer, his face bright.

"How do you feel?"

"Great, like I'm too amazing to mess up."

"What are you going to do the next time you feel you don't have a word?"

"Relax and wait on Him."

"And if you don't see or hear it?"

"I'll wait."

"Repeat after me: 'Holy Spirit, what should I do if I'm put on the spot and don't have a word or clear guidance?'"

Lucas repeated the prayer.

"What did you hear, sense, or see?"

"Holy Spirit said there will always be a word. I just have to train myself to listen to His voice and trust in Him."

"How does that make you feel?"

"Wonderful."

Lucas opened his eyes and shook hands with the Sozo minister. "Thank you."

"You're welcome."

Lucas's time with God was a breakthrough in connection with the Holy Spirit. Having judged himself for not bringing the person healing, Lucas had worn himself down with guilt and self-punishment. These contributed to a spiraling of lack of trust in the Holy Spirit that increased his fear of being inadequate as he stepped out to pray for others.

It is tragic how so many *Holy Spirit-filled* believers do not know God's presence. It has been our honor for the past 20 years to follow Bill Johnson, our senior leader at Bethel Church in Redding, California, in learning how to host God's presence. (For further research on this topic, read Bill Johnson's books, *Hosting the Presence* and *Face to Face with God.*) We have found that this inability to host His presence is one of the major problems for the Church today. Sozo works at healing all the disconnections between a person and God and removing any lies he has with his view of God and the truth of who He is as represented in His Word.

When we have confidence in our connection with God, we find ourselves better able to step out with the Holy Spirit's promptings and begin purposely affecting the world around us for His Kingdom. When we do not have relationship with the Holy Spirit, our ability to affect the world around us can be diminished.

In another example, a client named Tasha came in for a Sozo session to talk about her issues of not being close to Father God. The Sozo minister listened carefully and worked through the connection issues with the Father. As the session progressed, it turned out Tasha had a great connection with the Father. The minister brought this up, which confused Tasha at first. The Sozo minister asked if they could test the connection with the Holy Spirit.

At this point, Tasha physically moved back in her chair with a startled look on her face. The minister asked how she felt when discussing her relationship with the Holy Spirit. Tasha indicated she was not sure and resolved to work out her issues with Father God.

The Sozo minister suggested they remain with the Holy Spirit. Eventually, Tasha agreed. The minister had her forgive her mother for not being an area of safety. Tasha repeated the prayer and forgave her mother for any negative words she had spoken over her life. Finally, the minister had her renounce the lie that the Holy Spirit would also ridicule her the same way her mother had. After repeating the forgiveness prayer, Tasha opened her eyes and started to cry. She realized that that was the way she had always thought the Holy Spirit would treat her.

The minister asked if Tasha wanted to repent and see what the Holy Spirit actually had to say. Nervous, Tasha shifted in her seat but said she would try. Leading Tasha through the prayer, the minister asked Holy Spirit to interact with her and reveal truths. After waiting several moments, the minister asked what Holy Spirit had to say. Blushing, Tasha said Holy Spirit told her that He was not like her mother. The minister asked if Tasha believed what the Holy Spirit had said. Tasha was shocked. She could not believe that the Holy Spirit could be any different than she had believed Him to be. After working through some more lies, Holy Spirit imparted encouraging truths that Tasha had always wanted her mother to say. She started crying again. As she listened, Holy Spirit came closer until He asked if He could pick her up. Excited, she said yes.

When Tasha finally opened her eyes, she was smiling. She said she never realized that it was not Father God from whom her issues arose but rather the Holy Spirit. It comforted her to have this connection now for the first time.

Tasha's story shows the power of connecting to the Holy Spirit. Thinking her problems were with Father God, she discovered a new relationship with the Holy Spirit. Moments like these occur in Sozos often. Without having strong relationships built with each member of the Godhead, individuals are limited to what feels comfortable. We need to build strong relationships with each member of the Godhead so that we can begin to relate to God as He is and move beyond the confines of the familiar.

| Group Discussion Questions |

1. How do you see, hear, or sense the Holy Spirit in your life?

2. What are some places of fruitfulness in your life that are manifested because of your relationship with the Holy Spirit?

3. How was your relationship with your own mother growing up?

4. Do you need to forgive her for anything?

5. Do you need to renounce any anger, bitterness, or hatred you have toward her or other mother figures in your life?

| Activation |

1. Invite the Holy Spirit to come with His presence.

2. Thank Him for being the Comforter and Counselor.

3. Ask Him if there is any lie you are believing about Him and wait and listen for His answer.

4. Repent for believing any lies He revealed to you.

5. If necessary, forgive your mom or others for any way they have misrepresented the Holy Spirit to you.

6. Ask the Holy Spirit to reveal His truth to you regarding the lie you had believed.

7. Sever any ungodly demonic attachments that occurred because of believing these lies.

8. Ask Him to fill these vacated places with more of His presence.

| Suggested Materials |

Chapman, Gary. *The Five Love Languages: The Secret to Love That Lasts*. Chicago: Northfield, 1992. Print.

Johnson, Bill. *Hosting the Presence: Unveiling Heaven's Agenda*. Shippensburg, PA: Destiny Image, 2012. Print.

Johnson, Bill. *Face to Face with God: The Ultimate Quest to Experience His Presence*. Lake Mary, FL: Charisma House, 2007. Print.

Silk, Danny. *Loving Our Kids on Purpose: Making a Heart-to-Heart Connection*. Shippensburg, PA: Destiny Image, 2008. Print.

Chapter 7

DISEMPOWERING LIES

The Bible makes it clear where lies originate:

You are of your father the devil, and your will is to do your father's desires. He was a murderer from the beginning, and does not stand in the truth, because there is no truth in him. When he lies, he speaks out of his own character, for he is a liar and the father of lies (John 8:44).

In Scripture, the devil is described as the source of all lies. Seen as a roaming lion seeking whom he may devour, his three main purposes are to "steal, kill, and destroy" (see John 10:10).

The Bible shows that satan's goals are in direct opposition to God's. Rather than fruitfulness and connection, satan desires for us loneliness and separation. But Jesus, the Prince of Peace, crushes satan under His feet (see Rom. 16:20). By restoring God's truth to our lives, He disempowers the devil's schemes and empowers our destinies.

Scripture makes it clear that the devil has already been defeated. Throughout the Bible, God states His sovereignty over the "powers of this world." In the Book of Ezekiel, God recounts His authority over the fallen angel, lucifer:

Your heart was proud because of your beauty; you corrupted your wisdom for the sake of your splendor. I cast you to the ground; I exposed you before kings, to feast their eyes on you. ...All who know you among the peoples are appalled at you; you have come to a dreadful end and shall be no more forever (Ezekiel 28:17,19).

Nothing in this passage speaks of lucifer's strength. It shows satan, cast from Heaven, residing among the "peoples" of the earth to suffer their "appalled" glances. The Bible says satan was never meant to have dominion over the earth. God's punishment reduced him to powerlessness, a "dreadful end" that serves as an example of sin's consequences.

A theme that runs throughout Scripture is the truth that God wins. The Book of Revelation documents satan and his followers being thrown into the lake of fire (see Rev. 20:14). Because he is destined for destruction, satan's only hope is to deceive humanity. Doing this, he knows, hurts God's heart. Since he cannot touch the King, he attacks His sons and daughters.

Although satan has been defeated, his influence blossoms when humanity does not resist his lure. In the Garden, Adam and Eve gave him power when they submitted to sin. Doing this, they gave up their authority to rule and were banished from the Garden.

In Sozo, we recognize that for each one of us, God has created a destiny. It is our duty to steward its progression. Like Adam and Eve, we are commanded by God to be fruitful and multiply, to fill the earth, and to subdue it. In fulfilling our God-given roles, each of us, born with unique traits, giftings, and calls, expands His Kingdom.

Jesus makes stewarding our destinies possible. After the cross, Jesus took all authority from the devil. Ascending into Heaven, Jesus gave His disciples the Great Commission:

> *And Jesus came and said to them, "All authority in heaven and on earth has been given to Me. Go therefore and make disciples of all nations, baptizing them in the name of the Father and of the Son and of the Holy Spirit, teaching them to observe all that I have commanded you. And behold, I am with you always, to the end of the age"* (Matthew 28:18-20).

With Christ's mission accomplished, His assignment spread to the remaining disciples. Today, we continue this mission.

According to Christ, who sits at the right hand of God, we are no longer slaves to sin. If we realize this truth, the devil is unable to influence us with ungodly choices. It is only when we allow the devil a foothold that he becomes a serious problem.

Interestingly, even satan himself knows he has no true power. To convince people to follow him, satan may disguise himself as an angel of light. Doing this masks his schemes beneath the facade of "truth." Craftily, he veils his methods to appear beautiful and tempting. Otherwise, no one in his or her right mind would follow him.

Paul warns us of such tactics in Second Corinthians:

> *For such men are false prophets, deceitful workmen, disguising themselves as apostles of Christ. And no wonder, for even satan disguises himself as an angel of light* (2 Corinthians 11:13-14).

Paul points out a common tactic of evil: through deceit, the enemy appears benign. Remove his cloak of falsities, however, and we discover a dangerous adversary. Paul encourages us to practice discernment so we can distinguish who is with God and who is not:

> *But solid food is for the mature, for those who have their powers of discernment trained by constant practice to distinguish good from evil* (Hebrews 5:14).

Paul claims that maturity comes from practicing discernment. By increasing our ability to decipher what is God and what is not, we learn to identify the enemy's voice and dispel his thoughts. Instead, we can focus on the Lord's.

When we practice discernment, we see things through the Holy Spirit's perspective. His gaze, which pierces "bone and flesh, joint and marrow," reveals everything in its truest state (see Heb. 4:12).

As the teacher of discernment, Holy Spirit can unveil even the most disguised lies.

From years of Sozoing people, we have found that there can be any number of lies the enemy uses to imprison people. One way to categorize lies would be to divide them into three categories: *false truths*, *colored lenses*, and *crafty suggestions*.

False truths, which are ungodly reasonings posing as righteous beliefs, integrate into our belief systems and disrupt the flow of healthy living. When such lies sneak past our defenses, even the most powerful Christians can fall prey to their influences. These lies run rampant in the Church and mask themselves as righteousness, holiness, and even faith.

To understand an example of a false truth, we utilize the wisdom of Stephen De Silva, who runs the international ministry Prosperous Soul, where he explains that much of his early life was spent partnering with a mentality he calls the *poverty spirit*. Identifying this spirit as a mindset, Stephen asserts that believers who unknowingly partner with it appear humble, righteous, or godly. Sadly, doing so forces them to ignore the truth that they operate under the power of a lie.

An example of someone partnering with a poverty spirit can look like this:

Mark, a new Christian, decides to sell everything he owns to live in "righteous" poverty. He volunteers weekly at local soup kitchens. Not wanting to appear arrogant, he denies himself fashionable clothes. He begins to dress in simple, worn attire. It is not long before Mark begins punishing himself for thoughts of regret. He misses the days when he had something good to eat. He begins to miss the life he had.

After six months, Mark decides to re-evaluate his life. He applies to university, gets a degree in medicine, and starts a financially sound career. Now, out of his financial stability, Mark can donate money to those in need. This time, however, he is taking care of himself as well as reaching out to others.

Mark's case is extreme yet still conceivable. The poverty spirit masked itself as a form of "righteous" living. Because of his deception, Mark did not feel he was living the way God wanted him to. To be perfect, Mark believed he needed to deny himself the stability of money. While this may seem noble, the false truth of *money = ungodliness,* rather than the love of money being ungodly, was demonically inspired and could have permanently kept him from following his calling as a physician.

This can be why marriages, ministries, and lives fall apart. Seemingly harmless lies, which mask themselves as truths, sneak inside and find their ways into the corners of human thought. If individuals are not careful and open to accountability, they might find themselves victim to a demonic reality.

If you partner with a false truth, chances are you do not even know it exists. Most lies exist at a subconscious level. It takes God, revelation through the Bible, or a safe individual to point out a lie's existence. To help you understand more about false truths, here are some examples encountered through Sozo:

* Spirit of poverty: The Bible tells us to be poor (actually states "poor in spirit"), so God must not want me to have a lot of money. Therefore, I will not pursue a financially sound career.

* Lack of self-worth: I only carry value when I do something great for God. When I do not perform well for Him, I have no value.

* Self-loathing: Because of my past addiction to pornography, I cannot trust myself to be with only one woman. So I'd better not ever get married.

* False faithfulness: Since the Lord is coming back soon, I don't need to go to college or choose a career path. I just need to prepare for the end.

Each of these lies sounds righteous in a twisted way. However, if we partner with God's mindset, it is easy to see the devil's fingerprints. Each statement punishes the individual and drives him further from either God or the actual call on his life. This is a simple way to identify the difference between a truth and lie: Does the thought lead you to Christ? Does it spur you on to the call on your life? If not, then this thought is most likely from the one who wants to see you separated from God. Lies always lead to our own disconnection from God. Truth brings repentance and relationship.

Take Andrea's session with Rita as an example:

Rita, a senior Sozo minister, directed Andrea to her seat: "What brings you into a Sozo session today?"

Andrea took her seat and shifted uncomfortably. "I just want to be closer to God. I hear all the time about people who hear His voice and get direction, but I can never hear, sense, or see. Even when I read the Scriptures, He remains silent."

"Close your eyes. Ask Jesus if there are any lies you believe about Him."

Andrea closed her eyes and shook her head. "No. There aren't any lies. I know He loves me. There's nothing bad between us."

"Ask Him if there are any lies you believe about yourself."

Andrea took a moment to pray.

"No, I don't think so. I feel like I'm following Him wholeheartedly."

This example is common for those partnering with a religious spirit. This spirit tells us that *yes, God is good; and yes, He is all-powerful; and yes, we are to love and adore Him.* However, dealing with the religious spirit leads to incongruities. The person's need to hear God's voice is contrasted with the knowledge that everything is good. If everything was good, why would the person even bother to schedule a Sozo? Inconsistencies like this reveal the presence of a false truth. In this example, the religious spirit masked Andrea's disconnection with the lie that everything was good and in its right place.

At this point, Rita moved on and had Andrea ask Father God and Holy Spirit the same questions. If her answers did indicate an open door to follow, it would then be necessary to probe. Probing could look something like this:

"Repeat after me: 'I thank You, Father God, Jesus, and the Holy Spirit, that I am loved by You. But I forgive the church for training me to think that everything is all good between us even though You feel distant from me. I forgive the leaders in the church for not modeling a day-to-day closeness with You, Lord, and I renounce the lie that You won't talk to me today.'"

Andrea repeated the lie and began to cry. "He just seems so far away. I've been following Him for years and He still never seems close."

"Repeat after me: 'I hand to You the lie, Jesus, that You will always elude me. Jesus, what truth do You want me to know?'"

Andrea repeated the prayer.

"What do you hear, sense, or see?"

"Jesus says He is with me. Even when I don't see. He loves me and wants to communicate anytime I want."

"Repeat after me: 'I hand to You, Jesus, every lie I have believed about Your being distant. I renounce ties with any pride I have had in my perseverance to follow You even though You have felt distant from Me. What truth do You want me to know?'"

Andrea repeated the prayer.

"What's He saying?"

"He says He has always been here. And that He loves me."

"Repeat after me: 'I hand to You, Jesus, a religious spirit. What do You have for me in exchange?'"

Andrea began to cry some more. "He's giving me His presence."

In this example, the religious spirit's false truth separated Andrea from an intimate, personal relationship with God. On the surface, Andrea seemed quite spiritual. However, underneath she did not know how to access an intimate relationship with Him.

If you find yourself living under false truths such as self-loathing, poverty, false humility, or a religious spirit, renounce partnership with them and give them to God. Although years of partnering with such lies can make their practices seem congruent with Scripture, nowhere does the Bible support any of these counterfeits. This is why Paul states, *"Take every thought captive to the obedience of Christ"* (2 Cor. 10:5).

To renounce partnership with false truths, pray this simple prayer:

> *Father God, I ask You to forgive me for partnering with (insert lie here). I renounce partnership with this lie and any spirits attached to this lie, and I ask You to replace (insert lie here) with Your truth. I command the spirit of (insert spirit here) to leave me now in Jesus's name. Father God, what do You say as truth in exchange for this lie?*

After praying, wait to hear, see, or sense what God has in exchange for you. After receiving God's truth, thank Him for restoring you to freedom and put His gift to practice.

Whereas false truths can sneak past our defenses and fester in the church, *colored lenses* operate on a much wider scale. Affecting both Christians and non-Christians alike, colored lenses tint the way we see life. As examined in the first chapter, colored lenses result from partnering with a skewed perspective. These are viewpoints developed in childhood, most of them incorrect, which we embrace to cope with life's mysteries. When a parent or loved one hurts us, we construct realities to rationalize our hurt. We think that doing so helps us avoid repeated pain in the future.

Often, colored lenses are personal "truths" we have constructed through encounters with others. Sometimes conscious, lenses most often exist at a subconscious level. Like false truths, lenses can be identified by closely communicating with God, reading the Word, or interacting with others.

What we call "colored lenses" are ways of looking at life, people, yourself, and even God that skew the truth. We have found no limits to the array of colored lenses people wear. While some people partner with at least one colored lens, we have found that most individuals can wear multiple colored lenses, each of which affects their view of both man and God.

An example of someone partnering with a colored lens could look like this:

As early as Daniel could remember, he struggled with doubts about his intelligence. He had struggled with ADHD and dyslexia from a young age. Because of this, he had done poorly in school. Now Daniel was graduating high school. He was expected either to choose a university or begin a career. His parents urged him to further his education. In his heart, Daniel refused to believe he was smart enough to continue his education.

His parents, however, refused to give up. They prayed every day. Eventually, Daniel applied to a prestigious four-year university. To his surprise, he was accepted.

All throughout the application process, Daniel kept remembering his grades. In his heart, he knew he would never make the cut. Colored lenses of *I am stupid* and *There is no reason for me to continue* gnawed at his self-respect. It took a miracle and the support of his parents to overcome those obstacles.

Daniel went on to graduate magna cum laude. He continued his education at the same institution in pursuit of his master's degree. All of this would never have happened if he had listened to the lies, embraced the colored lenses, and given up.

Because colored lenses are so enmeshed with how a person thinks, it can be difficult to realize they even exist. As with false truths, many times it takes God's promptings, revelation through the Bible, or a safe individual to help point out a colored lens. To help in understanding more about colored lenses, here are some examples encountered through Sozo:

Victim Mindset:

1. Nothing is going to work out. Why try?

2. Everyone gets blessed but me.

3. My life will always be so hard.

Sadness/Discouragement:

1. People exist solely to disappoint me.

2. Sometimes it's just too hard to get out of bed.

3. No one understands me.

Fear/Self-Promotion:

1. If God is not going to promote me, who will?

2. I just don't carry enough of God's favor.

3. If I work hard enough, then God will promote me.

On the surface, each of these lies may sound absurd, but we rarely discern them as mindset lies because they have become our normal thought patterns. The only way for a person to discover if such patterns exist in his or her life is through relationship with healthy individuals and God and through studying the Word.

To identify a mindset's roots, ask the following questions: 1) Does this thought align with Christ's teaching? 2) Is this lifestyle leading me to or from God? If such mindsets bring disconnection from God, then you know they do not come from Him.

If you find yourself viewing life through ungodly perspectives, simple prayers can help to exchange such lenses for truth. Take Sally's prayer time with Dawna, for example:

Taking her seat, Dawna asked, "Why are you here today?"

"I've gotten such freedom in my life through Sozo but there is still one issue I cannot seem to break."

"What is it?"

"It doesn't matter who I'm with or where I am—whether I'm in public or attending a small group—I always feel no one wants me in the room. Even if someone acknowledges me, I just know they don't want me in the room."

At this point in the session, it was apparent that Sally partnered with a colored lens. Even though reality told her one thing (she was accepted), she refused to believe it.

Dawna chose to investigate.

"Let's ask Jesus where you learned this lie. Repeat after me: 'Jesus, where did I learn the lie that I'm not welcome at social gatherings?'"

Sally repeated the prayer. With a jump, she opened her eyes. "When I was three…"

"What do you remember?"

"I see myself almost three years old. I'm playing outside. I hear laughter coming from inside the house. When I open the door to investigate, everyone freezes. Immediately, the talking stops."

"Repeat after me: 'Jesus, what lie did I learn from this memory?'"

"That nobody wants me in the room."

"Ask Jesus for the truth."

Sally shifted in her seat. "He's showing me that it was the day before I turned three. My family and friends were planning to throw me a surprise party. When I walked in, they stopped talking because they didn't want me to find out."

"Repeat after me: 'I hand to You, Jesus, the colored lenses of rejection, isolation, and loneliness. I break off all demonic attachments to these lenses and I command any spirits attached to this lie off of me in Jesus's name.'"

Sally repeated the prayer. She looked up—smiling.

"How do you feel?"

"Accepted."

In Sozos, we find out how such lenses skew our clients' views of reality. We also find that clients typically have multiple skewed perceptions. It is very rare if a person does not partner with at least one colored lens.

Even the most wonderful parents fail to raise us perfectly. Innocent children, forever rationalizing, concoct strange and unbiblical reasons as to why certain things exist. If you find yourself partnering with colored lenses, do not panic. Work through the process with God, Jesus, or the Holy Spirit. Renouncing ties to a lens effect and receiving God's truth lead to freedom.

To renounce partnership with colored lenses, pray this simple prayer:

Father God, I ask You to forgive me for partnering with (insert lens here). I renounce partnership with this mentality and any spirits attached and ask You to replace (insert lens here) with Your truth. Father God, what truth do You have in exchange for me?

After praying, wait to hear, see, or sense what God has in exchange. After receiving God's truth, thank Him for restoring you to freedom and put this gift into practice.

The final category of lies we encounter in Sozo sessions can be seen as *crafty suggestions*. These are lies satan presents while disguised as an angel of light. They seem innocent at first; however, as we partner with the lie, a strong opposing spirit develops. To deal with this issue, believers must locate its source and dig up the root.

Notice how easily Adam and Eve gave in to the serpent's craftiness. On the surface, it looks as if satan questioned God's commandment not to eat from the tree of the knowledge of good and evil; however, his underlying message to Eve was to doubt God's character and motives toward her and the disallowed fruit. It may have looked to Eve as a question of whether God's commandment to them could really be trusted for their good. Tempted to act to fulfill their own needs and desires, rather that trusting God, Adam and Eve gave in to the serpent's suggestion. This one choice led to the Fall of Humanity.

Crafty suggestions start in the form of seemingly harmless ideas. Often, they take the form of temptation. These lies, if unaddressed, build from a small flame into an uncontrollable inferno.

An example of someone partnering with a crafty suggestion looks like this:

Ray, exhausted after a long day's work, plopped down in front of his computer to relax. His wife and kids, long in bed, allowed him a rare moment of silence. As he searched the online streaming sites for films to watch, he came across some that starred scantily clad actresses.

Ray moved his mouse to click on the link. *This is obviously not the wisest thing to watch*, he thought. *What would my wife think if I watched this movie?* Ray looked away from the screen. *It's not an adult film...it's just a harmless B-movie. I'll close my eyes during the raunchy parts.*

Ray returned his gaze to the computer screen. His fingers hovered above the mouse. *Why shouldn't I do it? It's harmless. It's just a stupid movie.*

Ray's toying with the lie of *It's harmless...it's just a stupid movie* made him vulnerable to following through on an ungodly act. This crafty suggestion took hold in his heart once Ray hesitated. Pastor Kris Vallotton, director of Moral Revolution, says the battle with sin is won in the mind. As soon as we begin to entertain the devil's thoughts, we have positioned ourselves for defeat. This is why the Bible tells us to "resist the devil" (see James 4:7). If we toy with his schemes, we lose.

To help illuminate the definition of a crafty suggestion, here are some examples encountered through the Sozo Ministry:

- Spirit of deception: If I am powerful, or since I hear from God myself, why do I need to listen to other people's advice?

- Lack of trust in God: I need money. God still has not come through. Maybe I should take matters into my own hands? I could always use the credit card.

- Lack of self-trust: I've failed too many times in the past. I'm going to have to find some other way to get a promotion.

Crafty suggestions work hand in hand with the spirit of deception. Coupling with dangerous mentalities, deception blinds individuals to the possibility of ever being wrong. It takes hard work and a willingness to repent for someone to renounce such partnerships.

Another example of someone partnering with a crafty suggestion looks like this:

Jake had been struggling with his marriage for years. Ever since their children had moved out, the distance between him and his wife had grown. Unresolved conflicts had heated to a boil. If any restoration were to be found, radical healing would need to take place.

Jake sat across from the Sozo minister, describing the effects of his painful marriage.

"I just don't care anymore. We've grown apart. She's not the same woman I married 24 years ago."

The Sozo counselor listened politely.

"Is there something specific you're wanting help with today?"

Jake crossed his arms. "I'm here because my kids would be devastated if it ended."

"Do you personally have any desire to see your marriage restored?"

Jake uncrossed his arms. "No."

"Well, then, you can either change your attitude and care about resolving your marriage or I can end this meeting now and save us a lot of heartache."

Jake shifted in his seat. "What do you mean?"

"It's clear that you're not interested in saving your marriage. The only reason Sozos work is because individuals want to receive healing. If you're going to make me work harder than you on your marriage, it's not going to be fun for either of us."

Jake paused. He mulled over his thoughts.

"What would you like to do?"

"I'm here. Let's give it a try."

"I can work with that. Why don't you begin with closing your eyes? Can you picture Jesus for me? What do you hear, sense, or see?"

Jake shut his eyes. He piqued his ears to listen.

"Jesus is standing across a large sea waving at me. We're miles away, but somehow I can see Him. I'm standing on the far side looking at Him."

"How does the picture make you feel?"

"I haven't felt close to Jesus in a long time."

"When's the last time you felt close to Jesus?"

"When my kids were young, my wife and I took them to Disneyland. We stayed there for three days. The girls had fun. My wife and I did, too. It was one of those rare occasions when everyone got along."

"Repeat after me: 'Jesus, what is it about this memory that You want me to know?'"

Jake repeated the prayer. He sat quietly in his seat.

"That it was fun. It was all about relaxing and spending time together."

"Repeat after me: 'Jesus, when did that change?'"

Jake repeated the prayer. Suddenly, his shoulders sagged. "When we got back home, my wife's parents were killed in a car accident. They had been using a car I had let them borrow. My wife always blamed me for it."

"How did that make you feel?"

"Sad and irritated."

"Repeat after me: 'I renounce the lie that I was responsible for the death of my wife's parents. Thank You that they were involved in our lives and contributed to our happy memories. I forgive my wife for holding bitterness against me. I release her from all guilt and judgment. And I thank You, Lord, for the fun we had as a family while on vacation. I forgive myself for not fostering fun in our home when we returned. I hand this all to You, Jesus. What truth do You have in exchange?'"

Jake repeated the prayer. The counselor gave him several minutes to respond.

"What do you hear, sense, or see?"

Jake's tense shoulders relaxed. "He said it wasn't my fault. I shouldn't judge myself. And the lack of fun is just as much her fault as it is mine. I need to stop blaming myself for everything."

"Repeat after me: 'Thank You, Jesus, for showing me that truth. Are there any more lies I'm believing about myself and my marriage?'"

Jake repeated the prayer. "That my marriage isn't fixable."

"You don't sound convinced."

"It's like telling me the Titanic will rise from the depths. I just don't see how it's possible."

"It might just be exactly what Jesus wants to do. Would you like to ask and see?"

Jake nodded.

"Repeat after me: 'I renounce the lie that my marriage is unsolvable. Thank You, Jesus, that You are the King of kings and Lord of lords. There is no task too great for Your wisdom and majesty. I ask You to forgive me, Jesus, for condemning my marriage. I hand it to You in Jesus's name and ask for grace and cooperation.'"

Jake repeated the prayer. He sat quietly in his seat.

"What's the Lord saying?"

Jake paused. He took a deep breath. "He says I need to stop being so bitter. It's time to move on."

"How does that make you feel?"

"I've been mad for a long time. If there was some way to cure it, I'd be interested."

"Why don't we hand this to Jesus and see what He thinks? Repeat after me: 'Jesus, I ask You to forgive me for holding onto bitterness. I release all anger, frustration, and bitterness. I forgive my wife for adding strain to our marriage by not communicating her needs. I hand to you the fear of impossibility and ask You, Jesus, to make all things new. Show me, Jesus, what I need to see. Jesus, what's the truth?'"

Jake repeated the prayer. The counselor allowed time to process.

"What's He saying?"

Tears welled in Jake's eyes. He wiped them away with a knuckle. "He says it's time to let go."

"Of your marriage?"

"My pain."

"All right. Repeat after me: 'Thank You, Jesus, for this call of surrender. I give up fighting to You and ask that You would take over and manage our relationship. I give You permission to bring our hearts together. I pray this all in Jesus's name.'"

Jake repeated the prayer.

"How does that make you feel?"

Jake composed himself. "Like I'm not dying."

"That's an improvement."

In Jake's scenario, his pain led him to partnering with the lie that his marriage was unsalvageable. Working through these lies, Jesus was able to break through Jake's doubts. Eventually, his tenderness was uncovered.

To renounce partnership with a crafty suggestion, pray this simple prayer:

Father God, I ask You to forgive me for partnering with (insert lie here). I renounce partnership with this deception from the enemy and ask You to replace (insert lie here) with Your truth. Father God, what truth do You have in exchange?

After praying, wait to hear, see, or sense what God has in exchange. After receiving God's truth, put it into practice.

Some may be discouraged when analyzing enemy tactics. In truth, there is no reason to be afraid. Jesus has already won. We find ourselves in the midst of a victorious battle. All we have to do is partner with Him to see it finished.

Jesus shows us how to demonstrate wisdom and power through partnership with the Spirit. By knowing who we are and to whom we belong, we, like Jesus, will not be swayed by the devil's logic.

Jesus displayed how to wage spiritual warfare when He resisted the devil in the wilderness. Rather than entertaining satan's thoughts, Jesus immediately responded to every temptation with God's truth. When satan told Jesus to turn stones into bread, Jesus responded, *"It is not good for man to live by bread alone"* (see Matt. 4:4). When the devil offered Jesus a shortcut to His promise, Jesus replied, *"You shall worship your Father God only"* (see Luke 4:8).

Jesus's strategy for combating satan's tactics was to respond with God's truth. He did not muse on the devil's thoughts. Instead, He reacted quickly, using the Lord's commandments to solidify His resolve. Like Jesus, Paul asserted stewardship over his thoughts:

We destroy arguments and every lofty opinion raised against the knowledge of God, and take every thought captive to obey Christ, being ready to punish every disobedience, when your obedience is complete (2 Corinthians 10:5-6).

The apostle Paul says that stewardship over our mind is key to becoming like Christ. By guarding ourselves against the enemy's thoughts, we permit righteous things to stay and contribute to the Lord's will. While discerning the enemy's voice can be difficult, having a heart aligned with God and His written Word allows for an easier identification of ungodly thoughts.

The response of Jesus to Peter in the Book of Matthew displays another example of swiftly identifying the devil's schemes. When confronted by Peter, Jesus responded with a rapid recognition of the spirit operating through His disciple:

> But He turned and said to Peter, "Get behind Me, Satan! You are a hindrance to Me. For you are not setting your mind on the things of God, but on the things of man" (Matthew 16:23).

Because Jesus was so aligned with God, He picked up on the devil's use of Peter. Jesus, always truthful, called His disciple out on what exactly was being communicated. Even so, their relationship was preserved.

This verse shows that Jesus, an expert identifier of the devil's lies, recognized His Father's voice and confronted anything that opposed it. If we long to live powerfully as Christ, we must train ourselves to hear God's voice and reject anything else.

If you find yourself entertaining thoughts presented by a seemingly harmless lie, renounce partnership and ask the Lord's forgiveness:

> Father God, I ask You to forgive me for entertaining destructive thoughts. I hereby renounce partnerships with any lies of the enemy and ask You to cleanse me from their effects. I hand these lies to You in Jesus's name. Father God, what do You have for me in exchange?

Write down what God says and put His truth into practice.

Whether you find yourself operating in false truths, colored lenses, or crafty suggestions, renouncing partnership remains important. If additional help is needed, schedule a Sozo session. Information on Sozo counselors residing in your area can be found on our website (bethelsozo.com).

After removing lies from your life, invite God's truth to take its place. His truths, which echo into eternity, bring healing, restoration, and hope. After receiving God's truth, you will experience a new level of peace in your life. It is then your job to walk out the healing and steward it to fruition.

Typically, after a Sozo session, we encourage clients to read through God's truths revealed in the session throughout the weeks following the breakthrough. Sometimes after a person receives truth he experiences thoughts that discourage his breakthrough. Whether psychological or spiritual, such encounters are harassments from the enemy. To counter this, reading over Scripture and God's truths recorded during the Sozo sessions will encourage the client to walk victoriously over the enemy's schemes.

Because Jesus prevailed, every sickness, lie, and hindrance is null and void. No perversion of the enemy has a right to exist. Jesus purchased abundant life when He died on the cross. We get to live fully because He took our pain. The prophet Isaiah records:

> *But He was pierced for our transgressions; He was crushed for our iniquities; upon Him was the chastisement that brought us peace, and with His wounds we are healed* (Isaiah 53:5).

Christ's wounds provide healing. He paid the price for our sins. We get to experience His breakthrough and live from the freedom of what He purchased.

To live successfully as a son or daughter of God, we must partner with His victorious mindset. To do this, we must equip ourselves as powerful individuals. Paul, in the Book of Ephesians, points out the necessity of adopting such practices:

For we do not wrestle against flesh and blood, but against the rulers, against the authorities, against the cosmic powers over this present darkness, against the spiritual forces of evil in the heavenly places (Ephesians 6:12).

Paul makes it clear that our enemy is not people. Our enemies are the *rulers, authorities, powers,* and *spiritual forces of evil in the heavenly places.* To combat the enemy, Paul admonishes us to put on the full armor of God. Doing so enables us to withstand satan's schemes:

Put on the full armor of God, that you may be able to stand against the schemes of the devil (Ephesians 6:11).

Stand therefore, having fastened on the belt of truth, and having put on the breastplate of righteousness, and, as shoes for your feet, having put on the readiness given by the gospel of peace. In all circumstances take up the shield of faith, with which you can extinguish all the flaming darts of the evil one; and take the helmet of salvation, and the sword of the Spirit, which is the word of God (Ephesians 6:14-17).

But the fruit of the Spirit is love, joy, peace, patience, kindness, goodness, faithfulness, gentleness, self-control… (Galatians 5:22-23).

Equipping ourselves with the Word of God, righteous faith, godliness, and the Holy Spirit, we align ourselves with God's truth. We are then able to withstand the enemy's attacks.

| Group Discussion Questions |

1. In reading through this chapter, did you identify with any of the types of lies mentioned (false truths, colored lenses, and/or crafty suggestions)?

2. Can you sense that there are some lies you are believing but are not sure what they are?

3. Ask the Holy Spirit to reveal to you what lies you have partnered with.

4. Ask the Holy Spirit what ungodly mindsets you have.

| Activation |

1. Close your eyes and ask the Holy Spirit if there is a lie or ungodly mindset with which you have been partnering.

2. Ask Him to show you where you first learned or partnered with this lie.

3. Ask Him to forgive you for believing in this lie and empowering it as truth.

4. Forgive anyone you feel helped teach you these lies.

5. Forgive yourself for partnering with these lies.

6. Ask God if there are any demonic attachments to these lies.

7. Renounce participation with any of these spirits and command them off of you in Jesus's holy name.

8. Ask Him what truth He wants to give you in exchange for the lies you have renounced today.

9. Invite the Holy Spirit to continue to walk with you through this season as you exchange your previous ungodly mindsets for His.

10. Ask the Holy Spirit to breathe into you understanding of His Word, the Bible, so that you are able to find in it the truths He has imparted to you today.

11. As you study the Bible, write out the verses that reinforce what He told you today.

12. Begin declaring aloud throughout your day the truth God has revealed to you until you *know* it is true.

| Suggested Materials |

Backlund, Steve. *Let's Just Laugh at That.* Redding, CA: Steve Backlund, 2011. Print.

Backlund, Steve. *Victorious Mindsets.* Redding, CA: Steve Backlund, 2008. Print.

De Silva, Stephen. *Prosperous Soul Foundations.* CD/DVD/Manual.

Johnson, *Bill. Strengthen Yourself in the Lord: How to Release the Hidden Power of God in Your Life.* Shippensburg, PA: Destiny Image, 2007. Print.

Johnson, Bill. *The Supernatural Power of a Transformed Mind: Access to a Life of Miracles.* Shippensburg, PA: Destiny Image, 2005. Print.

Martinez, Yvonne. *Prayers of Prophetic Declarations.* Redding, CA: Yvonne Martinez, 2013. Print.

Chapter 8

CLOSING THE FOUR DOORS

Lies tend to be the most common obstacles encountered in Sozo sessions. However, just breaking free of lies might not be enough for the client to achieve complete freedom. If the client has participated in sin, then the client must renounce the sin and ask for Jesus's forgiveness in order to break the demonic strongholds attached to the particular sin. When the Sozo Ministry began in 1987, the only tool we knew to use was Pablo Bottari's Ten Steps to Freedom. Since then, we have moved away from using the Ten Steps and have instead developed the *Four Doors*. This tool is used to identify strongholds in a person's life and to bring needed deliverance from demonic bondage. According to Bottari, a person's physical, spiritual, and emotional issues can be traced back to the opening of any one of these four doors: *fear, hatred/bitterness, sexual sin,* and *the occult*. Without using his method, Sozo retains the categories he identified as entrances in a person's life for the demonic realm.

In a Sozo session, ministers use the Four Doors to help identify sin in a person's life. Sozo ministers ask clients about these doors one at a time to discover the presence of strongholds. This process continues until the client feels that all four doors are closed.

The first and most frequently encountered of the doors is *fear*. Inside this door can be found *worry, unbelief, need for control, anxiety, isolation, apathy,* and *drug and alcohol addictions*. If a client struggles with any of these issues, the Sozo minister partners with the Holy Spirit to have the client renounce ties, ask forgiveness, and receive truth.

The process of dealing with the *Fear Door* can look like this:

Stacy, a single mom struggling financially, constantly battled with fear. While attending a Sozo seminar in Atlanta, Stacy volunteered to be part of a live demonstration. After coming up front and taking a seat, Stacy was asked by the Sozo leader to close her eyes and ask God where He wanted to start.

After several minutes, Stacy shook her head.

"What did you hear, sense, or see?"

"I just feel worried."

"About what?"

"My finances. Ever since my husband left, I've struggled to make an income."

"How does this worry make you feel?"

"Like I can't support my family."

"Would you like to hand it to Jesus? See what He thinks?"

"Yes."

"Repeat after me: 'Jesus, I hand to You apprehension, fear, worry, and stress. I refuse to allow those things a hold over my life. Forgive me, Jesus, for opening the door to fear. I ask You to sever all ties to demonic strongholds that were attached to these lies in Jesus's name. Jesus, what's the truth?'"

The Sozo minister allowed Stacy time to process.

"What do you hear, sense, or see?"

"Jesus is holding me and my girls. He says all the resources are available. All we have to do is ask. But we're in such a small house. It doesn't seem very safe."

"Repeat after me: 'I choose to forgive friends inside and outside of the Church for not helping in my situation. I release them from all judgment. I renounce the lie that I am alone and am unable to ask for help. I renounce ties with an isolated spirit. I hand these fears to You, Jesus, and ask You to remove all stress from my heart. Jesus, what do You want to give me in exchange?'"

Stacy repeated the prayer.

"What do you see, sense, or hear?"

"I see Jesus leading me through a library. He's turning on lights, dusting off books, and removing cobwebs."

"What does this picture mean to you?"

"Jesus said it's my heart. He just handed me a book. On the cover, it says *Old Dreams*. He dusted it off and said it's okay for me to dream again."

"Do you believe it?"

Stacy nodded.

"Great. Now close your eyes and see if you feel any other fear inside."

(After several seconds) "Yes. I see myself standing in the dark. Holding my arm. Like it's bruised."

"How does this picture make you feel?"

"Not safe. Like I've tried to be adventurous but failed."

"Repeat after me: 'I renounce any ties with fear of failure. I hand to You, Jesus, the lie that my past failures have crippled my ability to dream. I renounce the lie that I have to carry the things of my life alone. I hand the lie to You, Jesus, that my inability to do things perfectly results in punishment. Jesus, what's the truth?'"

(After several minutes of processing) "He said I was born to take risks. And that I'm not broken. I have His attention. I can come to Him whenever I have an issue."

"Do you believe it?"

"Yes."

"Repeat after me: 'Jesus, I ask You to forgive me for partnering with fear. I renounce partnering with a spirit of fear, and I command this spirit off of me in Your holy name. Please bolt this door shut so that it can't influence me anymore. What are You giving me, Jesus, in exchange for fear?'"

Stacy repeated the prayer. "He's giving me courage," she answered.

"Repeat after me: 'Holy Spirit, what do You want me to do when I start to feel afraid?'"

The counselor gave Stacy time to process. "What's He saying?"

"He says, 'Trust Me. I'll keep you safe.'"

"How do you feel?"

"Much better."

In this scenario, Stacy's worry, mistrust, and fear of failure needed to be replaced. Each kept the door to fear open and permitted the enemy's influence. To close this door, the minister led Stacy through repentance and exchange. Halfway through the session, Stacy forgave her friends for not helping financially. Whether it was their responsibility or not, Stacy felt abandoned. If she wanted to gain trust with Jesus, she needed to forgive those human relationships.

The underlying factors of Stacy's worry were isolation and fear of failure. Both kept her a victim of her circumstances. Because Stacy held on to her spiritual wounds, it was not until she refuted the lie of brokenness that she could see God's truth, which gave her permission to ask for help.

The truths instilled by God gave Stacy the comfort she needed to sever ties with fear. At the close of the session, the Sozo minister had Stacy ensure the door was closed.

(NOTE: Most times, Sozo ministers use the Four Doors tool until each area is shut. Only in cases where the client requires further sessions is a door left open.)

Following the *Fear Door* is the *Hatred/Bitterness Door*. Inside this door is *bitterness, envy, gossip, slander, anger,* and *self-hatred (low self-worth)*. This door can be confusing for Christians who believe it is impossible for believers to hate. The Bible certainly stands against it:

Everyone who hates his brother is a murderer, and you know that no murderer has eternal life abiding in him (1 John 3:15).

But I say to you who hear, love your enemies, do good to those who hate you, bless those who curse you, pray for those who abuse you (Luke 6:27-28).

With these verses in mind, is it possible for Christians to hate?

The answer is yes. Like Adam and Eve, we have the capacity to choose evil. God restored us as sons and daughters—this does not mean we are incapable of making poor decisions. Walking out our restoration is a mission all unto itself.

Since many Christians have difficulty reconciling with the word *hate*, ministers usually replace the word with *bitterness* or *unforgiveness*. We have found that unforgiveness, which manifests in hatred/bitterness and offense, stands as one of the greatest rifts in a person's well-being. When people hold on to anger, it invites the establishment of demonic strongholds. Paul speaks of this in Ephesians:

Therefore, having put away falsehood, let each one of you speak the truth with his neighbor, for we are members one of another. Be angry and do not sin; do not let the sun go down on your anger, and give no opportunity for the devil (Ephesians 4:25-27).

This is why the Bible commands us to forgive others. It not only benefits the person who has offended us, but it also delivers us from the offense held against us:

But I say to you that everyone who is angry with his brother will be liable to judgment; whoever insults his brother will be liable to the council; and whoever says, "You fool!" will be liable to the hell of fire. So if you are offering your gift at the altar and there remember that your brother has something against you, leave your gift there before the altar and go. First be reconciled to your brother, and then come and offer your gift (Matthew 5:22-24).

Closing the door to hatred and bitterness is inextricably linked to a person's ability to impart forgiveness. While sometimes it may be difficult to forgive, refusing to do so leads to negative fruit in our daily lives and to being locked up in a prison cell of our own design.

In one Sozo class, an older gentleman, Gary, came to the front to receive healing from arthritis. After Gary revealed his painful past as a Vietnam War veteran, the Sozo team leader decided to work through forgiveness.

"Close your eyes. Repeat after me: 'Holy Spirit, do I have any unforgiveness in my life?'"

"I don't have to ask. I know I do."

"What is it?"

Gary flexed his hands. "I served this country for years. For what? I'm a writer and can barely type."

"Repeat after me: 'Holy Spirit, who do I need to forgive?'"

(After a pause) "My country. I was treated like a murderer when I came back."

"Repeat after me: 'I choose to forgive my country for not honoring me on my return. I release any judgment in Jesus's name and forgive those who did not show me respect. I forgive those who labeled me as a murderer. I release all accusations in Jesus's name. Father God, what do You have in exchange?'"

Gary took a moment to process.

"What do you hear, sense, or see?"

"God said He was with me in the jungles. Keeping me safe. But if that's true, why didn't He protect my arms?"

"Would you like to see what Father God thinks?"

"If it helps."

"Repeat after me: 'Father God, what do You think of the arthritis? Why didn't You prevent that from happening?'"

After this prayer, Gary's countenance changed. "God said He's sorry for my arthritis. Said He knows how hard it's been but I don't need to be angry."

"Would you be willing to give Him the offense you have been carrying against Him?"

"Will He be mad at me? Do you think He will forgive me for being mad at Him?"

"We can certainly ask Him and see."

"If you think it'll help."

"It's always the Lord's will to heal. All we have to do is position ourselves for blessing. Releasing bitterness may help."

"Okay."

"Repeat after me: 'Father God, forgive me for holding bitterness against You. I remove all blame placed on You for the arthritis in my hands. I hand all arrogance, anger, and unforgiveness to You in Jesus's name. God, what do You have for me in exchange?'"

The minister gave Gary time to process.

"What do you see, hear, or sense?"

"God gave me a crown of righteousness. Told me I was always a prince in His Kingdom but now it's time to start acting like one."

"Do you believe that?"

"Yeah."

"Repeat after me: 'Father God, I hand arthritis to You. I give my body permission not to hold on to bitterness. I hand it all to You in Jesus's name.'"

Gary repeated the prayer. Feeling the Holy Spirit's presence, Gary buckled over. The minister asked how he was feeling. Gary flexed his hands.

"It's better."

"Repeat after me: 'Thank You, Father God, for this increase. We continue to ask for 100 percent.'"

Gary repeated the prayer and re-flexed his hands. The Sozo minister encouraged Gary to position himself for healing in the coming weeks. If any traces of bitterness arose, the Sozo minister encouraged him to give them up to Jesus.

In this scenario, Gary received a measure of healing. Though the healing was not complete, continuing to position himself for blessing could lead to an eventual release from arthritis. Certainly, his working through of forgiveness made way for the miraculous.

Interestingly, Gary's biggest victory was his release of judgment against the Father. Although this may sound unbiblical, Christians (as much as anyone else) can harbor anger against God. We believe this is some of what Paul calls *hardening our hearts* in the Book of Hebrews:

> As it is said, "Today, if you hear His voice, do not harden *your hearts as in the rebellion"* (Hebrews 3:15).

Releasing our judgments against both God and humanity are powerful ingredients in a person's physical or emotional healing. Although God is never truly at fault, clients build cases against Him that they need to release. The act of releasing bitterness against God allows the softening of hearts. In turn, this provides good soil for God's blessing.

After the *Door of Hatred/Bitterness* is the *Door of Sexual Sin*. This is the door that includes *adultery, pornography, fornication, lewdness, molestation, fantasy,* and *rape*. While committing sin against the physical body is the most socially unacceptable, the Bible makes it clear that entertaining lustful thoughts is equally dangerous:

You have heard that it was said, "You shall not commit adultery." But I say to you that everyone who looks at a woman with lustful intent has already committed adultery in his heart (Matthew 5:27-28).

Jesus's standard of sexual wholeness makes it necessary for us to live with the mind of Christ. To do this, we must deal equally with suppressed desires and actions.

Another danger of engaging in sexual sin is the formation of soul ties. Through sexual acts, spiritual and emotional attachments form. In marriage, these ties form healthy connections that create physical and emotional intimacy:

"Therefore a man shall leave his father and mother and hold fast to his wife, and the two shall become one flesh." So they are no longer two but one flesh (Mark 10:7-8).

We have found that soul ties are often created even outside of marriage. These soul ties can create unhealthy attachments. If left intact, residue from previous relationships can strain a present one.

To free oneself from an unhealthy soul tie, the partnership must be renounced and exchanged for God's truth. Renouncing a soul tie would look something like this:

Father God, I ask You to forgive me for engaging in sexual sin and creating an unhealthy soul tie with (person's name here). I ask You to forgive me and to sever any soul ties linked between me and (the person). I send back to (person's name) any part of him/her that I retained—washed through Your blood—and I take back any part of me that was left with (person's name)—washed through Your blood. Jesus, as You break this soul tie, what do You want me to know?

Even dabbling on the edges of sexual impurity can lead to unhealthy patterns. While conducting a Sozo seminar in Australia, a Sozo leader met with Nate, a middle-aged pastor, who confessed his ties with sexual sin. Though not engaged in the sins himself, Nate's relation to his brother, a distributor of pornography in the country, brought guilt and shame. Working with the team member, he confessed his need to forgive his brother and move on. However, Nate discovered some unturned stones in need of inquiry.

"Close your eyes. Repeat after me: 'Holy Spirit, is there any sexual sin in my life that we need to deal with?'"

Nate sat silently and crossed his arm. Chewing his lower lip, he admitted, "There is one thing."

"Go for it."

"I've always felt like I missed out. Like my brother gets to have all the fun while I sit it out. There's this nagging in me that thinks I won't ever have fun. Like I'm stuck in a religious institution while my brother lives one big extravagant party."

"Would you like to see what Holy Spirit thinks of that?"

"Please."

"Repeat after me: 'Holy Spirit, what is the lie I am believing?'"

Nate repeated the prayer. After a minute of silence, "That my life is boring. That I'd be better off in sin."

"Let's ask Holy Spirit for the truth: 'Holy Spirit, what's the truth You want me to know?'"

Nate repeated the prayer. After several minutes of silence, the minister checked to see if he was ready.

"I saw myself standing on a hill. Surrounded by light. Far off, I could see a realm covered in darkness. Holy Spirit said that was the realm of sexual sin. For miles, all I could see were people bent over and locked in chains."

"How does that make you feel?"

"Not too excited to join."

"Repeat after me: 'Holy Spirit, what do You think of my brother?'"

Nate repeated the prayer.

"I see Jesus holding my brother. Telling him there is another way. I asked Jesus if my brother would be all right, He said not to worry, the Holy Spirit would get ahold of him."

Nate's voice drifted off to a whisper. "He also said I have something beautiful. That although my brother's sin may look fun, that empire leads to sadness."

"Repeat after me: 'Holy Spirit, I choose to forgive my brother for making sexual sin look fun. I renounce the lie that I am confined to a boring life. I ask for fun to enter into my walk. And I ask for joy to fill every step. Holy Spirit, what do You want me to know?'"

Nate grinned.

"What did He say?"

"It's going to be a whole lot of fun."

Although Nate did not engage in sexual sin, his desire to taste its offerings pricked at his heart. Fortunately, these desires were dealt with before he took action.

If you find yourself partnering with sexual sin, or sneaking around to catch a glimpse of its offerings, repent and renounce partnership with it. No matter how far into sin you are, the Holy Spirit can always deliver you.

Take Teresa's client as another example of closing the door to sexual sin:

While the session was progressing, the client said he sensed the doors to sexual sin and hatred were open. Teresa asked the Lord if there was anyone the client needed to forgive. Listening, the client got the impression that he needed to forgive a friend who showed him how to "experience life" when they were teenagers.

He released forgiveness to the friend and to any others that continued in that lifestyle. He also forgave himself for choosing those actions to get his needs meet. He asked Father God if he was forgiven and Father God said yes. The client then asked Father God if there was anything else to be done to close the doors. Father God indicated that he needed to cut soul ties with those involved with sexual sin. Teresa led him through the cutting of soul ties, reclaiming what he had given away. Then Teresa commanded the spirit of perversion to leave in Jesus's name.

As Teresa declared these words, the client felt the doors close. Teresa asked him how he felt. The client said he felt complete for the first time in years.

The final of the Four Doors is the Door to the Occult. Inside this door is astrology, fortune-telling, tarot cards, séances, Ouija boards, manipulation, participation in covens, casting curses, and witchcraft practices. Even if a client never partners intentionally with these practices, purchasing items that may hold occult ties or a spouse's involvement in the occult can lead to demonic attachments.

This was the case for Mary, an attractive newlywed who attended a Sozo seminar in New Zealand. Having suffered extreme pain in her neck for years, she booked a session with one of the team members to gain deliverance. Accompanied by her father, Mary related her problems. When asked about her connections to the Door of the Occult, Mary confessed her and her husband's dabbling in past demonic experiences.

The Sozo team member led Mary through a simple deliverance prayer.

"Repeat after me: 'Father God, I asked You to forgive me for dabbling in the occult. I repent for investigating in these areas. I ask Your forgiveness in Jesus's name, and I break free in Jesus's name from any demonic spirits with which I partnered. Holy Spirit, what truth do You want me to know?'"

Mary listened for the Holy Spirit. She shook her head and placed a hand on her neck. "I can't hear anything. The pain in my neck is getting worse."

"Does it always get worse when you pray?"

"Sometimes."

"Holy Spirit, would You show me the source of this pain?"

At this point, the team member identified a demonic manifestation. He could tell it was not just a random neck ache. With the Holy Spirit's direction, he decided to investigate unhealthy connections with anger.

"Repeat after me: 'Holy Spirit, is there any anger in my life?'"

Mary repeated the prayer. Her eyes twitched. The team member took note of this and kept his expressionless "Sozo face."

"Yes, I do get angry. When I do, it makes me stronger. It's the only way I can defend myself."

Rejecting thoughts of fear, the team member continued, "Let's see what Holy Spirit has to say about that. 'Holy Spirit, what do You think about all this?'"

"He thinks it's bad. But I won't give it up."

At this point, Mary's voice had dropped several octaves. Her father, sitting in the corner, observed with enlarged eyes.

"Would you like to give that anger to Jesus?"

"No."

At this point, the team member decided it was best to take over the session.

"Holy Spirit, I ask You to invade this room and dispel all connections to the occult. I see you, enemy, and I laugh at your insignificance. Thank You, Holy Spirit, that You are more powerful than any demonic presence."

After the prayer, the demon's voice evaporated. Mary returned to her normal self.

"How are you feeling right now?"

"Good."

"Would you like to hand anger to the Holy Spirit?"

"Yes."

"Repeat after me: 'Holy Spirit, I hand to You all ties and connections to this anger. I ask You to forgive me for partnering with this spirit of rage. I renounce the lie that it makes me powerful. I hand it to You in Jesus's name. Holy Spirit, what do You have for me in exchange?'"

As soon as Mary repeated the words, she jolted and straightened up in her seat.

"It worked."

"What did?"

"My neck. There's no pain."

"None at all? Great. Let's thank Holy Spirit for intervening."

With tear-brimmed eyes, Mary rejoiced in the fact that this pain that had been with her for five years was suddenly gone.

In this example, a demonic spirit had attached itself to Mary's opening of the occult door. Masking itself as rage, the entity acted as Mary's defense in her hostile marriage. Whenever her verbally abusive husband would rage, she would turn on her ungodly ties to anger and frighten him into silence.

Her dabbling with occult practices permitted the demon to make itself a home. It was not until Jesus arrived and she confessed her sin and renounced agreement with it that the demon was forced to leave. Because Mary had given the spirit permission to stay, it would only leave once that permission was revoked.

A similar experience with the Occult Door occurred with Megan, a recent convert who had dabbled in the past with witchcraft. Arriving in Teresa's office, Megan begged for the session to deal specifically with closing the Occult Door. Someone had told her that she had a doorway open to the occult. Ever since then, strange things had been happening. To ensure the door was closed, Megan scheduled a Sozo. Teresa asked Megan if she had been involved in any occult practices growing up. Megan indicated that she had as a teenager.

When Teresa started to ask her how she perceived Father God, Jesus, or the Holy Spirit, Megan said she was afraid to talk with them because she felt they would be upset with her past occult practices. To remedy this, Teresa led Megan in a prayer of renunciation.

"Repeat after me: 'I renounce the lie that because I dabbled in past demonic experiences, Father God, Holy Spirit, and Jesus will not talk to me. Father God, what's the truth?'"

Megan repeated the prayer. Ensuring her client had time to process, Teresa waited several moments before continuing. When she felt Megan was ready, Teresa continued, "What do you see, sense, or hear?"

Megan frowned. Teresa asked what she was experiencing.

"I see all these people laughing at me—the ones who introduced me into the occult activities."

Seeing a need for forgiveness, Teresa led her through a quick prayer. Hesitantly, Megan forgave those who invited her into the occult world. Following this, she forgave herself for thinking the demonic realm could meet her needs. Teresa led Megan through a prayer of release and had her renounce any ties that could connect her to the Door of the Occult.

As Megan repeated the prayers, Teresa could tell something was happening. She asked Megan what she could hear, sense, or see. Megan said she saw Jesus close the door and was shocked that Jesus cared enough to do it for her. He then stood in front of the door and told her He would not allow anything to enter.

Megan cried and thanked Jesus. Teresa asked if she believed Jesus' act. Megan said yes. She left the session knowing her demonic harassment would end.

When discussing the Door to the Occult, it is important we do not give the enemy unnecessary power. The Bible states the enemy has no authority over us at all:

> *And Jesus came and said to them, "All authority in heaven and on earth has been given to Me"* (Matthew 28:18).

The Lord, infinite in size and power, can, has, and will crush the devil. In addition, we are called to *"crush satan under our feet"* (see Rom. 16:20). It may be necessary to remind the client that the fight between God and satan is not equal.

In working through a demonic deliverance, we have found that the enemy will try to coerce ministers and clients into fear. In stirring up fear, the demonic realm feigns strength. The best way to reduce its feigned power is to ignore its attempts at intimidation. Dawna says that demons are like puffer fish. They expand with taunts and threats—even physical manifestations—but the name of Jesus is more than enough to puncture their expansion.

After closing the Four Doors, the Sozo minister has the client check with the Holy Spirit to ensure there is nothing else to be worked through. If nothing is revealed, the doors are assumed to be closed.

| Group Discussion Questions |

1. Do you feel like there is any unforgiveness or bitterness you have toward anyone?

2. Do you sense that you need to forgive yourself?

3. Do you have an offense against God for things not going right in your life?

4. Do you sense that you carry any fear?

5. Are there any sexual sins you need to renounce?

6. Were you ever involved in any occult practices?

| Activation |

1. Ask the Holy Spirit if there is anyone you need to forgive.

2. Release forgiveness to anyone with whom you are angry or from whom you have experienced hurt.

3. Ask God to break any ungodly soul ties to these individuals.

4. Once you finish forgiving, hand to God all bitterness, hatred, and anger.

5. Ask Him what He wants to give you in exchange.

6. Ask Father God to reveal to you if you have any fear, worry, or anxiety in your life.

7. Ask Him to show you where you first encountered fear.

8. Release forgiveness to anyone who opened this door to you.

9. Repeat steps seven and eight until you feel you have addressed all your fears.

10. Ask God to forgive you for partnering with fear.

11. Command fear to leave in Jesus's name.

12. Ask Him what He wants to give you in exchange for fear.

13. Ask Him to close the door to fear.

14. Ask the Holy Spirit to reveal any unpardoned sexual sin you still need to renounce.

15. Ask Jesus to forgive you for partnering with sexual sin.

16. Break all soul ties to partners with whom you had sex before you were married.

17. Break all soul ties to any partners that were not your spouse with whom you had sex while married.

18. Send back any part of him or her that you retained because of the soul tie.

19. Ask God to give you back any part of you that you left with these partners.

20. Hand to Father God perversion, shame, and guilt.

21. Command any demonic attachments to leave.

22. Ask Jesus what He wants to give you in exchange for shame, guilt, and perversion.

23. Ask Him to close the door to sexual sin.

24. Ask the Holy Spirit to reveal any openings to the occult. (Do not be surprised if He brings up something seemingly unrelated. Go ahead and follow His promptings.)

25. Ask God to forgive you for anything He reveals.

26. Renounce participation with anything He reveals.

27. Forgive anyone who opened this door to you.

28. Renounce partnership with anything you participated in that gave power to the enemy in your life.

29. Ask Father God to come and cleanse you from all ungodliness.

30. Ask Him what He wants to give you in exchange.

| Suggested Materials |

Blatchford, Faith. *Freedom from Fear* CD/DVD.

Bottari, Pablo. *Free In Christ: Your Complete Handbook on the Ministry of Deliverance*. Lake Mary, FL: Creation House, 2000. Print.

De Silva, Dawna and Teresa Liebscher. *Sozo Basic*. CD/DVD/Manual.

Chapter 9

SHIFTING ATMOSPHERES

Kevin Spacey's famous line from the film *The Usual Suspects* goes: "The greatest trick the devil ever pulled was convincing the world that he doesn't exist."[1] We have found that so many Christians live with a belief that since God is good—which He is—then there is no need to pay attention to the demonic realm. We have found this to be an extremely dangerous position for the Church to take.

When we ignore the truth of God and satan, Heaven and hell, and angels and demons, we believe ourselves to be masters of our own fate. Sadly, we fail to realize our theology's consequences. By ignoring the presence of God, we become vulnerable to evil. When the Church fails to present sound teaching on both God and the enemy, we create space for the world to intervene with its own view of the supernatural. Thus, Hollywood films are filled with both good and bad vampires, good and bad witches, and good and bad demons. This blurs the lines of truth and anesthetizes the minds of unbelievers and believers alike to the evil around us.

Whether we like it or not, the world is engaged in a spiritual war. There is a God and devil, a good and evil, a Heaven and a hell. While the Lord seeks to bring life and impart destiny and identity, the devil longs to steal, kill, and destroy. Fortunately, we already know who wins:

And the devil who had deceived them was thrown into the lake of fire and sulfur where the beast and the false prophet were, and they will be tormented day and night forever and ever (Revelation 20:10).

And although we know that God wins over satan in the end, Paul discusses the reality of our spiritual war here on earth in Ephesians:

For we do not wrestle against flesh and blood, but against the rulers, against the authorities, against the cosmic powers over this present darkness, against the spiritual forces of evil in the heavenly places (Ephesians 6:12).

Fortunately, earlier in Ephesians we are told:

He worked in Christ when He raised Him from the dead and seated Him at His right hand in the heavenly places, far above all rule and authority and power and dominion, and above every name that is named, not only in this age but also in the one to come (Ephesians 1:20-21).

And raised us up with Him and seated us with Him in the heavenly places in Christ Jesus (Ephesians 2:6).

According to Paul, evil (although lesser than God) is present and resides in heavenly places. Broadcasting messages of hate, sin, and slavery, evil can easily brainwash those who refuse to guard their minds.

As Christians, we are called to partner with God to see His Kingdom reign. Because the blood of Christ redeems us, we stand victoriously. Warring against evil, then, becomes not a burden or heavy lifting but simply a matter of partnering with Him to see His victory complete.

Taking inspiration from Ephesians, Dawna teaches a concept called *Shifting Atmospheres*. In her teachings, she describes the practice of identifying enemy *broadcasts* over a person, place, or region. Broadcasts of the enemy can be messages of hate, sin, slavery, immorality, or whatever else the devil wants to impart. This is why Dawna believes certain individuals, regions, and places seem to carry specific mindsets or lies that need to be replaced with God's presence.

To shift atmospheres, Dawna proposes a person first needs to identify the enemy's broadcasts. Once identified, the broadcasts can be ignored, deflected, or stopped. An *atmosphere* is the overall "feel" and "sense" of a place. This is why Dawna believes that certain homes, people, and territories "give off" specific vibes. These atmospheres can most easily be compared to listening to a specific radio station.

It is important to note that not all atmospheres are demonic. Think of the last time you went to see a movie. Going into the theater, did you bring preconceived notions of what the film was about or come in with a poor attitude and see your personal atmosphere shift from frustration to joy?

Maybe you had a rough time at work. Perhaps you showed up at the theater buried in a cell phone, trying to forget the day's frustrations. Either way, once the movie started, your personal atmosphere was replaced with a sense of adventure, thrill, and awe. This is something most audiences experience when seeing *Star Wars* or *Raiders of the Lost Ark* for the first time.

Yet another famous film that shifts atmospheres for viewers is the famous *Jaws*. To this day, millions hear the score by John Williams while swimming and fight the fear that tells them to get out of the water.

To better understand the concept of atmospheres and how to identify them, consider these questions: 1) Have you ever entered a room, met a person, or crossed over into a new state or country and suddenly felt different physically, emotionally, or spiritually? 2) Did you enter your workplace feeling sad only to perk up moments after? 3) Perhaps you woke up this morning in a good mood, then as your day progressed, slid into a mild case of depression?

If you have experienced any of these instances, chances are you encountered a change in atmosphere. As you practice discernment, you will be able to see how atmospheres "broadcasted" from people, places, or regions can influence how you think, feel, and behave. As an empowered Christian, you do not have to be afraid or come under these thoughts or feelings. If you find yourself partnering with or experiencing an atmosphere, repent and renounce partnership with it and ask God what He would like to impart in its place.

Dawna experienced this firsthand while on a ministry trip to another country. During the middle of her first night, Dawna and her younger son, Timothy, both experienced a violent dream. In her dream, Dawna spent the night barely escaping being attacked and raped. When she went to Tim and Cory's room the next morning, Timothy recounted his night's dreams of continually rescuing women from acts of violence. Rather than partnering with fear, she brought these feelings to God. Later, she discussed this with her son and remaining team members.

It turns out that during the night, several other Sozo team members had experienced similar dreams. This confirmed Dawna's intuition that this was a sign of an atmosphere of sexual violence that was rampant in the area. When Dawna approached the church's senior leaders about the dream, both leaders confirmed that the area experienced a high rate of abuse.

Partnering with God, her team, and the senior leaders over that area, Dawna renounced ties with domestic abuse. She invited the senior leaders to ask for the Lord's forgiveness for the region's agreement with sexual violence and sought the Lord for what He wanted to put in its place. After praying, she and the senior leaders released peace, health, and protection of women over the region.

Upon her return to the area a year later, the church leaders reported a decrease in violence in that region. Fortunately, Dawna and her team had used what the enemy broadcasted to identify the attack. They then partnered with God to reverse its effect. The city pastors have had such a noticed impact in that area that a local school asked them to come and simply be present on the school grounds after school was released so that the same peace would be released over the school grounds.

Notice that in this story, Dawna and her team members did not come under the negative atmosphere or give it authority. Instead, they used what they picked up in their dreams as information to determine the enemy's attack. Bringing this possible broadcast to the team and senior leaders, they were able to impart God's opposing spirit of peace, protection, and wholeness. Because of this tactic, a community began to change.

This is the goal of shifting atmospheres. As believers, it is our job to dispel darkness and to be the light Jesus called us to be to this world. Discerning atmospheres is not meant to scare you. You do not have to come under the broadcasts of the enemy and give them spiritual authority. If we stay elevated and in tune with God, hearing or seeing the enemy's plans can give us strategy. When the enemy shows his cards, we know his next play. We can then partner with God to see how to reverse the enemy's plans.

We suggest you journal your thoughts, emotions, and experiences throughout the day to identify spiritual atmospheres in your region, home, or workplace. Record them over the course of a week. See what a "normal" experience is for you. Do not include moments of crisis. Only document moments that occur regularly. You will see a pattern emerge and understand what sort of atmosphere you give off. Dawna's workbook, *Atmospheres 101*, would be a great resource for you while you practice picking up and displacing the atmospheres around you.

The more you pay attention to the broadcasts, the more your discernment will improve. As you identify places in town and/or people that emit certain atmospheres, you will be better equipped to partner with God and ask Him what He wants to release into the atmosphere to combat the existing broadcast. Then, through prayer, you can partner with Him and see it displaced.

Changes in atmospheres can either be subtle or dramatic. They can occur sneakily in the form of *I-thoughts* (e.g., *I am such a loser* or *There is no way I am getting that promotion*) or hit us like a full force of resistance. For the subtler approach, you might find yourself in a group of people feeling confident, then experience thoughts of self-doubt (e.g., *I am so ugly. I'm not wanted. I don't belong. What am I doing here?*). Such thoughts resemble ones we would usually embrace as our own. It will be difficult to recognize and identify those coming from an atmosphere outside our own. However, if we watch ourselves carefully and realize when such thoughts are not part of our normal mindset, we can easily see the devil's handprint.

The hardest atmospheres to identify are the ones that sound normal to us. These are atmospheres that correspond to our own internal mindsets that we have partnered with for years. Bill Johnson, when preaching about the disciples and Jesus sailing in a tremendous storm, states, "You will only have authority over the storms you can sleep through." (See Luke 8:24.) In short, when we partner with fear in our own lives, we will have little authority over an atmosphere of fear.

To discover if we partner with any negative mindsets or atmospheres, look to Scripture. John 10:10 shows us that the devil's intentions are to steal, kill, and destroy. Therefore, any thought, feeling, or attitude that steals from, kills, and destroys us has its origins from him instead of God. God's plan to silence these enemy broadcasts is simply to think on blessed things: *"Whatever is true, noble, just, pure, lovely, good report"* (see Phil. 4:8). It may take some time to readjust what tape your mind plays, but it is crucial to replace these mindsets with God's truth.

Whereas personal atmospheres can be easily displaced, strongholds exist at a deeper level. Strongholds develop over time as a person submits to an enemy's regime. They allow the devil's hold to strengthen through repetitive agreement with his broadcasts. Often, strongholds can be passed down through generational agreements to long-held family beliefs that are inconsistent with God's Word.

However strongly held, a stronghold's power, we believe, can also be quickly removed when the person who submitted to its authority takes ownership for his sin, asks God's forgiveness, and walks without further agreement with it. After confessing his sin of agreement with these strongholds, he needs to replace prior mindsets with God's truth. Although the process is similar to replacing lies, resistance against strongholds tends to be more intense. Sozo ministers encourage clients to go after a stronghold only once they have fully determined to see it overthrown and replaced by the Holy Spirit. This caution comes from a warning in Luke:

> When an unclean spirit goes out of a man, he goes through dry places, seeking rest; and finding none, he says, "I will return to my house from which I came." And when he comes, he finds it swept and put in order. Then he goes and takes with him seven other spirits more wicked than himself, and they enter and dwell there; and the last state of that man is worse than the first (Luke 11:24-26 NKJV).

Only after completely renouncing partnership with it, opening ourselves to being filled with God's truth and His Holy Spirit, and fostering a desire to change sinful patterns do we stand a chance of full recovery.

Strongholds can take root several different ways. One is by opening any or all of the Four Doors. For example, when people practice sexual sin, they invite the demonic to partner with them in their sexuality. If they continue to operate in this opened door, a stronghold of perversion can attach to them.

Another way a stronghold is developed is through generational patterns and lifestyles that are passed from parents to children. If a child is raised in a home where the parents yell and rage at him, the child can see this as a normal form of parenting and can carry this into his own family later in life. If a child grows up in a home with molestation, the child will not understand proper boundaries and may later grow up to partner with a stronghold of sexual sin.

A stronghold is broken via the process of forgiveness, repentance, and renunciation. As we allow God's Spirit to displace a stronghold's authority, this stronghold can be broken. However, because strongholds are developed over time, a person's walk into complete healing may also take some time. Whereas the renunciation and initial deliverance can be instantaneous, keeping the open door closed will be the client's job outside of a Sozo session. Through continued agreement with God's truth and obedience to it over time, strongholds are replaced with proper lifestyle choices. More about this is included in chapter 12.

As listed in Ephesians, the most authoritative of all demonic atmospheres are *powers* and *principalities*. These are spiritual realities assigned to messages broadcast over a specific region. These need to be shifted for God's Kingdom to increase, but they usually cannot simply be dealt with like a stronghold or lie. Through years of agreement by those living in the region, they have been given authority. To displace their power, Christians need to communicate with God and see His plans for the area. Of course, God always wants cities, people, and regions delivered. However, going after a spiritual power outside of a person's realm of authority is not only unwise but unbiblical.

In the Bible, a group of exorcists learned the importance of getting permission from the Lord. Without checking with God, they undertook a deliverance for themselves. Unfortunately, it did not go so well:

Then some of the itinerant Jewish exorcists undertook to invoke the name of the Lord Jesus over those who had evil spirits, saying, "I adjure you by the Jesus whom Paul proclaims." Seven sons of a Jewish high priest named Sceva were doing this. But the evil spirit answered them, "Jesus I know, and Paul I recognize, but who are you?" And the man in whom was the evil spirit leaped on them, mastered all of them and overpowered them, so that they fled out of that house naked and wounded (Acts 19:13-16).

Revivalist David Hogan, who ministers deep within the jungles of Mexico, encounters many regional powers and principalities. Some of these manifest themselves physically. David maintains that to combat these and serve on his ministry team, a person must have raised at least one person from the dead.

Why such strict admittance? David understands the importance of authority. The enemies he encounters in the jungles of Mexico have held authority for years—possibly centuries. He understands that to be protected by God, his ministers need to show they have been given authority in the spiritual realm.

This does not mean the enemy has more power than God. It simply shows a spiritual hierarchy in the atmosphere. To protect ourselves during warfare, we need to ensure we have both the Lord's blessing and His timing. Riding out into battle without His covering can bring retaliation from the demonic realm.

The wise and biblical method of dealing with a power or principality is to displace it through prayer. Francis Frangipane, in *The Three Battlegrounds,* writes, "We can all cast out demons, but we displace regional spirits."[2] Displacing an authority is usually not an instantaneous occurrence. It begins with identifying its presence, renouncing any participation with it in the past, committing not to partner with it in the future, and releasing what God planned for the area in its place:

*If My people who are called by My name humble themselves,
and pray and seek My face and turn from their wicked ways,
then I will hear from heaven and will forgive their sin and
heal their land* (2 Chronicles 7:14).

A great book for prayer strategies is Beni Johnson's *The Happy
Intercessor.* It is worthwhile reading for those who have struggled under
the weight of intercession in battling the demonic realm.

Here is an example of someone who did not follow these
steps successfully:

(NOTE: The story below is not meant to instill fear. It is included
to show the importance of following God's heartbeat. Like Jesus, we
should only do what we see the Father doing.)

*So Jesus said to them, "Truly, truly, I say to you, the Son
can do nothing of His own accord, but only what He sees
the Father doing. For whatever the Father does, that the Son
does likewise"* (John 5:19).

June, recently saved, recognized a negative spiritual presence residing in a house she had been living next to for over 15 years. As a new
believer, she was learning the importance of spiritual warfare. Excited
by the possibility of testing out her theories, June decided to visit the
house and cast out its authority.

June forgot to ask and see what the Lord wanted her to do. She
arrived at the house the next day and commanded the demonic presence to leave. After declaring it to leave, June's courage faded. The
grace she thought she had disappeared. Suddenly, an intense feeling
of fear came upon her. Fearing for her life, she sprinted home and
slammed the door. However, the sense of fear lingered. Over the following weeks, she experienced severe night terrors, to the point of
having to schedule a Sozo session for deliverance.

In the session, June quickly experienced freedom. The Sozo minister
asked one simple question: "Did you ask God if you had permission?"
Obviously, June had not thought of this. She repented for acting out

of ignorance and not asking God what He wanted her to do about the house next door. Working through some lies with the minister, June discovered that God had not assigned her the responsibility to see the house delivered. Instead, He wanted her to pray and wait for His instruction. Leaving the session, June experienced a new measure of freedom and a greater regard for listening to the Father for direction.

God enjoys partnering with us for the redemption of the earth. However, that does not mean the salvation of the world is on our shoulders. We have found that for our clients, unhealthy responsibility is just as dangerous as refusing to follow the Lord's voice. Shifting atmospheres can be safely accomplished by seeing what the Father is doing, staying under His wings of protection, and releasing His attributes and desires into the atmosphere to dispel the existing powers and rulers there. We are to identify what is being transmitted, see what God wants to do about it, and release His presence. Sometimes He will have us do nothing. Other times He will tell us to act immediately. Let Him be in charge of any spiritual warfare. It will keep you directly under His authority and in His peace.

NOTES

1. *The Usual Suspects*, directed by Bryan Singer (1995; Hollywood, CA: MGM, 2006), DVD. (NOTE: We are not endorsing this movie, simply quoting from it. It is not one we recommend.)

2. Francis Frangipane, *The Three Battlegrounds: An In-Depth View of the Three Arenas of Spiritual Warfare: The Mind, the Church and the Heavenly Places* (Iowa: Arrow Publications, 1989).

| Group Discussion Questions |

1. Do you know what your "normal" personal atmosphere is?

2. Do you lose your peace when you are with a lot of people or are in other places?

3. Do you know of the broadcasts that people around you are releasing?

4. Do you know of any strongholds in your life?

5. Do you know the broadcasts you are releasing?

6. Have you discerned the powers or principalities over your region?

| Activation |

1. Ask Father God to show you the personal atmosphere you give off to others around you.

2. Repent for any ungodly atmospheres you have been releasing.

3. Ask Him where you learned a lie with which you agreed that opened a door to your releasing this specific atmosphere.

4. Forgive anyone who hurt you as you learned this lie.

5. Hand the lie to Jesus. Ask Him what truth He has for you in exchange.

6. Ask the Holy Spirit what new atmosphere He wants you to release from now on.

7. Make a commitment to begin walking out this shift and to release God's heart throughout your day.

| Suggested Materials |

De Silva, Dawna. *Atmospheres 101*. Redding, CA: Dawna De Silva, 2013. Workbook.

De Silva, Dawna. *Shifting Atmospheres*. CD/DVD.

Johnson, Beni. *The Happy Intercessor*. Shippensburg, PA: Destiny Image, 2009 Print.

Vallotton, Kris. *Spirit Wars: Winning the Invisible Battle Against Sin and the Enemy*. Bloomington, MN: Chosen Books, 2012. Print.

Chapter 10

DISPLACING THE ORPHAN SPIRIT

There is an old quote that says, "all roads lead to Rome." In the realm of inner healing, all lies, fears, and strongholds lead to satan. God has twice as many angels as satan has demons, yet the world is in turmoil. How is this? The answer is simple: the world is partnering with an orphan spirit.

Joseph Mattera, the presiding bishop of Resurrection Church in New York, sheds light on the meaning of this phrase:

> Ever since Adam and Eve were alienated from God the Father in the Garden of Eden, an orphan spirit has permeated the earth, causing untold damage! (By "orphan," I am referring to a sense of abandonment, loneliness, alienation and isolation.) Almost immediately after the fall in Eden, the fruit of this orphan spirit resulted in jealousy, culminating in Cain murdering his brother Abel because God the Father didn't receive Cain's offering. To make matters worse, in contemporary society, with the breakup of the nuclear family, large amounts of people are not only alienated from God but are brought up without the loving care and security of their biological fathers.[1]

The orphan spirit embodies the mindset of a son or daughter separated from his or her loving Father. Out of this sense of abandonment, lies, sin, and selfish acts flourish to medicate the loss of identity, provision, and protection. When we overlay this truth with biblical knowledge, we see how this concept is multiplied because of a lack of daily communion with our Heavenly Father.

Stephen De Silva maintains that the orphan spirit, like the poverty spirit, is not a demon. Rather, it is a mindset. "If the orphan spirit was a demon," he proposes, "casting it out would instantly bring freedom." However, through Prosperous Soul Ministries, Steve has found that removing the orphan spirit works only when connecting individuals to the Father's heart. Through this encounter, clients can renounce partnership with the orphan spirit's mentality and accept Christ's spirit of adoption. (See Romans 8:15.)

What is Christ's spirit of adoption? It is the Father's spiritual adoption of His sons and daughters. It is what we receive when we enter the Kingdom through accepting Jesus's sacrifice for us on the cross. It is the gift Adam and Eve squandered when they sinned against God in Genesis. Being a spiritual son or daughter brings unity with the Father. It breaks off the lies we are believing, shows the truth of our identity, and gives us the courage to powerfully walk out the individual call on our lives.

Since the Fall of Man, God the Father began to propose a way to restore His sons and daughters to their previous relationship with Him—one of walking unashamedly with Him in a place of great peace. He went so far as to offer His precious Son, Jesus, as a living sacrifice to redeem fallen man. Giving Himself as the blood-price for humanity, Jesus rose again as the eternal and powerful Son. With His ascension, we were offered the chance to re-access a personal relationship with our Father: *"And the curtain of the temple was torn in two, from top to bottom"* (Mark 15:38).

After salvation, Christ's spirit of adoption is the next step the world needs to take in order to solve its tumultuous problems. As well as escaping hell through salvation, we can empower the world to supplant the orphan mindset by experiencing deep individual connections with the Father. Just imagine a world connected to the Father and filled with a restoration of identity, peace, and joy.

This is why Paul tells us not to conform to the pattern of the world (see Rom. 12:2). The world—steeped in an orphan mindset—binds itself to a temporal existence focusing on earthy substitutes to alleviate the stress of mortality. Instead of focusing on the world's fleeting existence, Christians have the option to live with eternity in mind. This allows us not to get pulled into ungodly sensual desires and to make choices that benefit those around us rather than just ourselves. At Bethel, we call this *Kingdom living*.

> *Do not be conformed to this world, but be transformed by the renewal of your mind, that by testing you may discern what is the will of God, what is good and acceptable and perfect* (Romans 12:2).

> *Pray then like this: "Our Father in heaven, hallowed be Your name. Your kingdom come, Your will be done, on earth as it is in heaven"* (Matthew 6:9-10).

To break free from the orphan spirit, we must accept Christ's spirit of adoption. To do this, we need to renounce ties with the orphan mindset and accept God's truth.

The process of identifying, renouncing, and replacing the orphan spirit follows a similar process to that of renouncing a lie. Since it is a mindset, we may need outside sources to help us discern that these thoughts are in opposition to the cross.

To better identify the orphan spirit, here are some of its fingerprints:

1. I am alone: I hate it when others succeed. It makes me look bad.

2. I am unwanted: I have to take care of myself. No one's going to care for me.

3. I am unworthy: If I want love, I need to earn it.

4. I have to self-medicate: There is nothing wrong with me. I just need to keep working. The pain will take care of itself.

5. I have worth only when I am a success: If I succeed in my career, I will finally gain approval.

6. Other people are just objects for me to use: I have to make the most of my relationships. People are a necessary step to climb.

Thought processes such as these signify traces of the orphan spirit. They are lies designed to keep people feeling afraid, isolated, and apart from God. This leads to a fear of lack in provision, protection, and identity.

Someone who struggles with the orphan spirit may look like this:

Doug, who was in his 30s, was an aspiring writer. Time spent with his wife and two daughters, however, left little time for creative exploration. His two closest friends, Caleb and Trent, decided to start a weekly writing group, and Doug could only make two of these meetings per month because of his schedule.

As time went on, each participant's writing skills increased. Doug, however, saw more improvement in Caleb's and Trent's work. He felt it was because of their more flexible schedule that they were able to put more time into writing. The results seemed unfair to him. His own skill grew at a slower rate.

Doug's first hint of jealousy occurred at a local open mic night. Reading his poems aloud, Doug noticed his amount of applause was lower than the rest of the contestants—especially Caleb's and Trent's. To alleviate this, Doug threw himself deeper into his writing. Determined to improve, he declined invitations for parties with his children. He even ignored the occasional date nights he and his wife had set aside.

Sure enough, Doug's skill began to grow. However, Caleb and Trent were still ahead. They were also receiving interest from publishers. The crushing blow hit when a local publishing company offered Caleb and Trent publishing deals, ignoring the manuscript he had sent along with theirs.

Caleb and Trent, of course, were ecstatic. Doug, on the other hand, was devastated. In the coming months, Caleb and Trent found themselves getting more and more favor with the local press while Doug continued to feel himself slipping away. Slowly, he began to resent his two friends. Doug, rightly or not, felt abandoned.

Unfortunately, Doug never communicated his feelings. Because of his pain, Doug began to drift apart from Caleb and Trent. Their writing partnership dissolved. Out of despair, Doug decided to abandon his writing altogether. It was only after his wife, Colleen, found his manuscripts in the trash weeks later and encouraged him to keep going that Doug found himself dreaming again. Eventually, he submitted a manuscript to a local film production office and received a call-back.

In this scenario, Doug's resentment of Caleb's and Trent's success signified partnership with the orphan spirit. Driven by the need for success, Doug valued himself only when he felt on equal terms with his friends. Because of his anger at their success, he secretly wished for them to be torn down. Every time their skills improved, Doug felt that much smaller.

Doug's scenario is a typical expression of the orphan mentality. When partnering with an orphan mindset, one begins to hear internally such thoughts as the following: *I can't succeed. I won't be able to do this. I am not as good as other people. I will not ever be favored like they are. He is taking my place on stage. I just have to work so much harder to do well than those who have natural, God-given talent.* These voices are in direct opposition to a Kingdom mentality.

When partnering with the orphan mindset, one begins to attach to such spiritual components as competition, jealousy, envy, hatred, and anger. Entertaining these voices over time builds into us ungodly strongholds. Paul warns us about partnering with these thought patterns:

> *But now you also, put them all aside: anger, wrath, malice, slander, and abusive speech from your mouth* (Colossians 3:8 NASB).

These attitudes are in direct opposition to conforming to the image of Christ and work to put us against one another. This is one reason the orphan spirit is so dangerous. When people walk as orphans, they believe that there is never enough. Having no connections to how the Father sees their realities, they begin to grasp for their own promotions and success. This causes squabbling with others, further alienating them from those around them. Dawna believes in two distinct types of behavior categorized by the orphan spirit: she states that disempowered orphans act as victims and empowered orphans act as bullies.

While it is easy to see the orphan mentality in a person carrying out a victim mindset, many people misunderstand the origins of the mindset of a bully. Whereas people carrying a victim mindset can be ridiculed as weak, bullies can be celebrated as powerful or successful. Other attributes of a powerful orphan could include performance, perfectionism, and an ungodly measure of self-sufficiency. These can sometimes allow a powerful-looking orphan to hide the underlying mindset of an orphan spirit.

To be rid of the orphan spirit, we must accept our adoptions as sons and daughters of God. The process of renouncing partnership with the orphan mentality and accepting Christ's could look as follows:

Carol, a recent grandmother, came into the center. After welcoming two new grandchildren into her life, Carol experienced severe depression. Not knowing what it was attributed to, she scheduled a Sozo session. When she arrived, the team member noticed an unhealthy attachment.

"What is it you need prayer for today?"

"It seems so silly. I just welcomed two new grandkids into my life. I should be thrilled. But all I feel is sadness and depression."

"Have you ever experienced this before?"

"Never this bad."

"Would you like to ask Jesus to come join us and see what He thinks?"

"Wholeheartedly."

"Close your eyes. Repeat after me: 'Jesus, are there any lies I am believing about myself?'"

The minister allowed Carol a few minutes to process.

"Let me know what you hear, sense, or see."

"I see myself as an infant in the hospital. My mother is holding me."

"How does this make you feel?"

"Good. But I remember this is the last time my mother ever saw my dad. Shortly after this, he left. We never saw him again."

"Can we pray something together?"

"Of course."

"Repeat after me: 'I choose to forgive my dad for abandoning us, for not being our provider and protector, and for not even being in my life growing up. I renounce the lie that I am not worthy of being a daughter. Father God, what truth do You want me to know?'"

The minister handed Carol a box of tissue, which she quickly used. The minister gave her several minutes to process.

"What did Jesus show you?"

"He said my father's absence is not a sign of my lack of value. It just means he wasn't there."

"I see. Would you mind if we try praying something?"

"Please."

"Repeat after me: 'Jesus, I renounce the lie that my grandchildren will not have access to a loving father.'"

At this, Carol began to cry. She wiped tears from her face.

"Repeat after me: 'I repent for believing the lie that my son-in-law will abandon their kids.'"

Carol finished drying her eyes. She crumpled the tissue in her hands.

"And I forgive my son-in-law for reminding me of my father."

Carol repeated the prayer. She wiped her nose with the tissue.

"Father God, is there anything else attached to this lie that we need to deal with?"

After several moments, Carol shook her head. She opened her eyes.

"I never realized how much of my dad I saw in my son-in-law. He's nothing like him, but I've always had issues trusting him."

"We can work on that. Would you like to see what Jesus thinks?"

"Yes."

In this Sozo session, Carol struggled with the orphan spirit. Because of her father's abandonment, she had no concept of what a healthy father-child relationship looked like. To cope with her pain, she transposed her fears onto her son-in-law and attached a fear of abandonment onto her two grandchildren. To receive peace, she replaced mistrust with God's acceptance. Once Carol renounced ties with her fear, she could see things from Heaven's perspective.

After she worked through several more lies, her depression lifted. She reported months later that she could enjoy her grandkids without fearing they would be abandoned. For Carol, her Sozo session was a great success in accessing God's spirit of adoption.

NOTES

1. Joseph Mattera, "The Difference Between the Orphan Spirit and a Spirit of Sonship," *Charisma News* (27 April 2013), accessed 31 January 2016, http://www.charismanews.com/opinion/the-pulse/39229.

| Group Discussion Questions |

1. Do you see any fingerprints of the orphan spirit in your life?

2. Do you struggle with unhealthy competition?

3. Do you struggle to celebrate other people's successes in areas where you need breakthrough in your own life?

4. Do you feel isolated, rejected, or lesser than others?

5. Do you feel superior to others around you?

6. Do you overwork yourself to earn approval or success?

7. Do you identify yourself more as a powerless orphan?

8. Do you feel you are the subject of prejudice in your work or school?

9. Do you feel like you just cannot get a break in life?

10. Do you find yourself grumbling at the hand that life has dealt you?

11. Do you feel like people treat you with a measure of disrespect?

12. Do you identify yourself more as a powerful orphan?

13. Do people see you as a mean, demanding person?

14. Do people experience you as aloof or rude?

15. Do you sometimes see yourself as better than the people around you?

| Activation |

1. Ask the Holy Spirit to reveal to you any fingerprints of the orphan mindset in your life.

2. Ask Him to show you whether you carry more of the victim or bully aspect of the orphan spirit.

3. Write down what He reveals to you.

4. Ask Father God to forgive you for acting out of these mindsets.

5. Ask Him to forgive you for partnering with any of the lies you have been believing about yourself as an orphan.

6. Renounce agreement with the orphan mindset.

7. Hand Him the orphan mindset with which you have been partnering.

8. Ask Him what truth He wants to give you in exchange.

9. Ask the Holy Spirit for a first practical step in changing your previous behavior.

10. Write down what He tells you and practice this throughout the week.

| Suggested Materials |

De Silva, Stephen. *Prosperous Soul Foundations.* CD/DVD/Manual.

Frost, Jack. *Experiencing Father's Embrace.* Shippensburg, PA: Destiny Image, 2002. Print.

Chapter 11

LIVING IN HEALTHY BALANCE

Scott," Dave called, "I need you to get those crates from the warehouse ASAP."

Scott bent over the wheel of his forklift. "I've got to make sure this works first."

"Fix it tomorrow." Dave tapped his clipboard with a forefinger. "Right now I need you to transport crates."

"Ouch!"

Scott scraped his knuckle on a bolt. Irritated, he smashed his wrench against the tire. Dave examined his watch.

"You finished?"

Scott stared at his bloody hand. Thoughts rattled in his mind. *Doesn't he care that I cut myself?*

"Scott, are you listening?"

Scott's rage boiled. He was no longer seeing Dave but his uncaring father, Glen. He began to clench his fists.

"Scott. Scott!"

Dave tapped Scott's shoulder. "You awake?"

Scott snapped back to reality, fingers tightening over his wrench. Slowly, he began to calm down. *Everything's fine*, he thought. *The work's going to get done. The boss needs help. I just need to relax.*

"Scott?"

Scott mulled over truths in his mind. *I forgive my dad for lashing out when things were tough. I renounce the lie that You, Father God, won't protect me. I hand fear of abandonment to You in Jesus's name. Holy Spirit, what's the truth?*

"Earth to Scott."

Scott looked at Dave. He laid down his wrench.

"You going to do what I ask?"

"I'll be right over."

"Good. Report to Jameson when you get there."

Dave turned to leave.

On his way to the warehouse, Scott processed his heart's turmoil. *I'll never get to work for a safe boss*, he thought. *Why did Father God put that clown above me?* Pausing in the hallway, Scott prayed: "Holy Spirit, show me Your truth."

Instantly, Holy Spirit showed Scott a vision of himself as a boy. His father, Glen, stood over him, reprimanding him for his lack of good grades. In the midst of pain, Scott managed to squeak: "Where were You, Father God?"

Holy Spirit continued with the memory. Scott saw himself, age twelve, covered in tears as his dad humiliated him—crumpling the report card and throwing it in the trash. Father God appeared beside Scott and whispered, "Scott, you're not stupid."

Back in the present, Scott bent over. He wiped tears from his eyes. At 37 years old, he never had been told he was intelligent. Messages from his earthly father were always geared toward his lack of stellar grades. But the message now from Father God was assuring him that his intelligence was not in question here.

Humbled and transformed, Scott stood and continued his trek to the warehouse. Thoughts of lack and shame were far behind.

In this scenario, Scott's willingness to seek truth from God made it possible for him to avoid an explosion of rage. It enabled him to step past his employer's rudeness and carry out his assignment. Although the communication between him and his employer needs some work, Scott's commitment to taking his thoughts captive enabled him to act wisely.

Imagine what Scott's situation might have looked like had he not used his relationship with the Holy Spirit.

Scott scraped his knuckle on a bolt. Irritated, he smashed his wrench against the tire.

Dave examined his watch. "You finished?"

Scott stared at his bloody hand. Thoughts rattled in his mind. *Doesn't he care that I cut myself?*

"Scott? Are you listening to me?"

Scott's rage boiled. He was no longer seeing Dave but his uncaring father, Glen.

"Scott!" Dave tapped Scott's shoulder. "You awake?"

Out of reflex, Scott grabbed Dave's wrist and twisted it. Dave screamed and collapsed to the floor. Scott stood over him, nostrils flaring. A few more screams and Scott snapped back to reality. He let go and retreated several steps. Nursing his wrist, Dave struggled to his feet.

"Clear your locker. You're through..."

"Dave...I didn't..."

"Out."

Scott dropped his wrench. He sprinted to his locker. Dave's pained groans followed him as he left.

In working with clients through the years, we have found that unresolved offenses can trigger our emotions, often irrationally, in certain situations. Such is the case with Scott's example above. His past experiences with his angry, impatient father triggered his explosive reaction to his demanding boss. In the prior example, taking every thought captive prevented him from lashing out and losing his job. Later, as he left for the warehouse, he was able to take some time to process his emotions and discover God's truth about himself rather than respond negatively to his boss. Doing this inner talk allowed him to achieve a sense of closure and peace.

Obviously, the first of these two interactions is a better demonstration of how to stay away from believing a lie. The fact that Scott's scenario involved a painful trigger did not help. In the first scenario, Scott used his relationship with the Holy Spirit to elevate his gaze above hurtful memories of his father. This allowed him to think rationally and escape the tyranny of his past trauma.

In the second situation, Scott partnered with rage. Rather than bringing his situation to God, he surrendered to it. In the process, his relationship with his boss, his job, and his reputation suffered.

Many people live like Scott in the second scenario. Even if an individual does not react violently, he or she may still give power to a false thought. Passive-aggressive behavior can be just as damaging to a relationship as a loud, boisterous attack.

Here's another example that shows a more passive (and perhaps more common) exchange:

Katie, who recently graduated from a university, decided to visit her friends in Redding, California. After driving the eight hours from Hollywood, she discovered her friends were not at the house ready for her arrival. Unable to reach them, she took a trip to the local health food store. Standing in the aisle, she contemplated her friends' absence. *I can't believe they didn't wait up for me. Don't they know I just drove for eight hours?*

Suddenly, Katie's phone buzzed. She looked at the screen. Heather's name appeared.

"Katie," Heather said. "I just got your text. We're out at the Rosen-hall downtown. You want to join?"

"I was kind of hoping you'd be at the house. I've got some things to unload."

"Sure thing. I can send my brother, Zack, over to help. We should be there in about forty minutes."

"What's going on?"

"Some party for a friend. She's about to return home. I'm so sorry we weren't there. I'll try to speed things up and be there as soon as I can. You're not upset, are you?"

"Of course not," Katie said, her fingers whitening over the phone as her grip tightened.

"Thanks for understanding..."

Katie hung up.

An hour later, Heather and her roommates arrived. Angrily lay-ing her things on the couch, Katie wrapped herself in a sleeping bag and closed her eyes. Heather, seeing Katie asleep, motioned her roommates away.

This scenario, as silly as it sounds, represents common communica-tion. Katie, unable to guard the thoughts in her mind, took offense at Heather's lack of communication. She ended her night with anger—something the apostle Paul warns against:

> *Be angry and do not sin; do not let the sun go down on your anger, and give no opportunity to the devil* (Ephesians 4:26-27).

Although Heather created an issue by not telling her friend she would be late, Katie had no right to build a case against her. In this example, Katie allowed herself to take the role of a victim by refusing to communicate her feelings. As the victim, she justified carrying the offense against her friends.

Here is what the same scenario looks like through a victorious lens:

Standing in the aisle, Katie contemplated the absence of her friends. *I can't believe they didn't wait up for me. Don't they know I just drove for eight hours?*

Suddenly, Katie's phone began to buzz. She looked at the screen. Heather's name appeared.

"Katie," Heather said. "I just got your text. We're at the Rosenhall downtown. You want to join?"

"No, thanks. I was hoping you'd be at the house. I've got some things to unload."

"I can send my brother, Zack, over to help. We can be there in about forty minutes."

"Heather, I'm sorry if this sounds harsh but I just drove eight hours and was excited to see you. It would mean a lot to me if you came to the house yourself and let me in. I'll consider the party, but I need to get settled first."

(After a pause) "I can do that."

"Thank you so much. By the way, what's going on?"

"My friend's going away party. She's leaving town. Just came up out of nowhere. I decided to go on the fly."

"Well, thank you for rescuing me. It means a lot."

"I'll be right over."

Katie hung up.

In this example, Katie exercised good boundaries and acted according to biblical truth. Instead of believing possible lies of not being valued or not being cared for, she acted out of her God-given identity that she was safe, beloved, and protected. Doing so enabled her to communicate her needs more effectively to her friend.

Both Katie's and Scott's decisions to combat lies with truth enabled them to rise above their situations. Like Jesus, they did not allow their circumstances to dictate how they behaved. Instead, they kept their core truths intact while navigating conflict.

This is key for anyone desiring to live victoriously. Even the most difficult situations can be opportunities for breakthrough. Jesus depicted this in the Gospel of Luke:

> *One day He got into a boat with His disciples, and He said to them, "Let us go across to the other side of the lake." So they set out, and as they sailed He fell asleep. And a windstorm came down on the lake, and they were filling with water and were in danger. And they went and woke Him, saying, "Master, Master, we are perishing!" And He awoke and rebuked the wind and the raging waves, and they ceased, and there was a calm* (Luke 8:22-24).

Where each disciple saw a fearful storm, Jesus saw an opportunity to release God's peace. God will always give you an opportunity to turn your situations to good.

Jesus perfectly illustrates God's design for the Christian life. Created to expand His Kingdom, we are called to prosper inside and outside of the storms of this world. Whether we face a heated conversation or a natural disaster, God has placed in us the capacity to stay above it and impart His truths:

> *And we all, with unveiled face, beholding the glory of the Lord, are being transformed into the same image from one degree of glory to another. For this comes from the Lord who is the Spirit* (2 Corinthians 3:18).

The Spirit, who reveals His glory, brings transformation. As we encounter His presence, we become more like Him. Taking the time to examine our growth is beneficial. And as we grow, we move from glory to glory, conforming daily to the image of Christ.

| Group Discussion Questions |

1. Are there any areas in your life that you find yourself still struggling to overcome?

2. Do you have any outbursts of anger?

3. Do you find yourself frustrated at the way other people treat you?

4. Do you punish people by withdrawing from them when you feel hurt by them?

5. Do you keep yourself at a distance from others to feel safe?

| Activation |

1. Ask the Holy Spirit to reveal to you if you still carry any offense.

2. Ask Him to reveal how these offenses affect your daily life.

3. Ask Him whom you need to forgive and then release forgiveness to them.

4. Ask Him what He wants to give you in exchange for your prior behavior.

5. Ask Him to ignite in you a love for His Word.

6. Ask Him what is the next step He wants you to take in your process of conforming to the image of Christ.

| Suggested Materials |

Farrelly, Dann. *Brave Communication*. CD.

Silk, Danny. *Keep Your Love On: Connection, Communication & Boundaries*. Redding, CA: Danny Silk, 2013. Print.

Chapter 12

WIELDING THE WEAPON
OF OBEDIENCE

In Chapter 11, we examined how healthy individuals interact when introduced to conflict. In this final chapter, we want to look at how people preserve the breakthroughs they receive. In the Sozo Ministry, we suggest the answer exists in the often misunderstood principle of obedience. For the purpose of this chapter, "obedience" will be defined as *following the requests of a law or person in authority.* "Authority" will be defined as *a person or organization having power or control in a particular, typically political or administrative, sphere.* However, in the world today, obedience tends to be seen as an act of subservience rather than honor. While we are taught to obey our parents, teachers, and leaders, some in authority do not inspire our trust or confidence. In instances of abuse, children grow up to believe the lie that obedience is an act of weakness. Out of fear of being controlled, abused individuals shield themselves from opening up to potential leaders.

Scripture commands us to respect authority and act with obedience:

> *Obey your leaders and submit to them, for they are keeping watch over your souls, as those who will have to give an account. Let them do this with joy and not with groaning, for that would be of no advantage to you* (Hebrews 13:17).

In addition, the Bible makes it clear that authorities exist because God allows their presence:

Let every person be subject to the governing authorities. For there is no authority except from God, and those that exist have been instituted by God (Romans 13:1).

If you find yourself having a hard time obeying leaders, you may want to ask the Holy Spirit to reveal the presence of any colored lenses through which you are seeing leadership. You may find that the reason you see leaders in a negative way is that your perspective is "tuned" to that logic.

Obedience is critical to the Body of Christ. Jesus, the Author and Perfecter of our faith, served as the ultimate practitioner of obedience:

So Jesus said to them, "Truly, truly, I say to you, the Son can do nothing of His own accord, but only what He sees the Father doing. For whatever the Father does, that the Son does likewise" (John 5:19).

Jesus submitted to the Father's will even when it led to sacrifice. His life demonstrated a continual act of servanthood. Matching His level of obedience is the goal for all Christians. To accomplish this, we need to develop a deeper relationship with Him. When we realize His plans for us, it is easier to follow through with difficult tasks:

And now, behold, I am going to Jerusalem, constrained by the Spirit, not knowing what will happen to me there, except that the Holy Spirit testifies to me in every city that imprisonment and afflictions await me. But I do not account my life of any value nor as precious to myself, if only I may finish my course and the ministry that I received from the Lord Jesus, to testify to the gospel of the grace of God (Acts 20:22-24).

Submitting to God's plan allows us to access our individual callings. Like Paul, we use obedience as our shield when faced with difficult moments.

An often misunderstood aspect of obedience is its ability to be used as a weapon of spiritual warfare. This is why James encourages us to "submit fully to God." By giving ourselves to the Lord, we reject any opportunities of agreement with the devil:

> *Submit yourselves therefore to God. Resist the devil, and he will flee from you* (James 4:7).

The Bible says satan *"prowls around like a roaring lion, seeking someone to devour"* (1 Pet. 5:8). To avoid being devoured, we need to resist the enemy.

Sin is described in Genesis as a hungry presence waiting for people to partner with its schemes. God warned Cain of the importance of mastering it:

> *The Lord said to Cain, "Why are you angry, and why has your face fallen? If you do well, will you not be accepted? And if you do not do well, sin is crouching at the door. Its desire is for you, but you must rule over it"* (Genesis 4:6-7).

Obedience to Christ leads to having authority over sin. As stated earlier, Bill Johnson teaches, "You only have authority over the storms you sleep through."

Ephesians 6:12 tells us there are *"rulers, authorities, powers, and spiritual forces of evil"* in the heavenly places that we struggle against (Eph. 6:12). How do we survive the onslaught of attacks? Part of the answer was discussed in James 4:7. The rest of the ingredients are found in Ephesians 6:

> *Finally, be strong in the Lord and in the strength of His might. Put on the whole armor of God, that you may be able to stand against the schemes of the devil. For we do not wrestle against flesh and blood, but against the rulers, against the authorities, against the cosmic powers over this*

present darkness, against the spiritual forces of evil in the heavenly places. Therefore take up the whole armor of God, that you may be able to withstand in the evil day, and having done all, to stand firm (Ephesians 6:10-13).

Sometimes submission is the only way we outlast the enemy's strategies. Pastor Kris Vallotton of Bethel Church states that the devil flees difficult battles because he lacks the fruits of the Spirit, specifically patience. Therefore, one way of usurping his attacks is to simply wait him out. Here is a verse to read over yourself in such times:

For this light momentary affliction is preparing for us an eternal weight of glory beyond all comparison, as we look not to the things that are seen but to the things that are unseen. For the things that are seen are transient, but the things that are unseen are eternal (2 Corinthians 4:17-18).

Standing in the face of the enemy's opposition is a form of obedience to God. Believing God's faithfulness pulls you through.

Dawna experienced this firsthand when confronted with the reality that a habit she had partnered with for years turned out to be ungodly. Growing up, she learned that no matter how difficult a day had been, she could rely on her dreams at night to make her "feel better." In her dreams, she could forget stress, inadequacy, and things of unimportance. Laying her head on her pillow, she could instantly be off on adventures. She cherished these dreams and even looked forward to extra naps in difficult times.

One day, while having lunch with her good friend, Renee, Dawna realized her sin. Renee noticed that today Dawna seemed unusually tired. When Renee asked why, Dawna said that she had not gotten enough sleep the night before because she was in an amazing dream. She explained that when lying down, she could let her brain take her into numerous adventures. These dreams, like movies, lasted throughout the night.

Renee, with concern, said, "I can't do that." Dawna said, "Wow. You must have boring dreams at night." Renee replied, "Actually, I have God dreams all the time." At this point, Dawna realized something was wrong. In her spirit, she could tell the dreams she had been partnering with for the past 20 years were not God dreams. Renee went on to say that Dawna's partnering with these dreams represented a spirit of fantasy.

Dawna received this like a slap to the face. She sat back and thought, *Oops. Bummer for me.* In truth, this was not a fun revelation. Dawna had grown to cherish this aspect of her life. The voices calling to her at night had comforted her since childhood. While she saw it as a necessary tactic of distraction, it had become a form of escape from daily discouragement. Not until God used Renee's insight did Dawna realize the depth of her deception.

At that moment, Dawna repented and asked God's forgiveness. She renounced partnership with the spirit of fantasy and asked for God's rest in exchange. During the weeks following, Dawna renounced its calling each night. Because she had partnered with it for so long, its presence had become a stronghold. To diminish its power, she had to renounce its temptation over the next few months. Finally, she began to lay her head on her pillow and not feel its draw. This victory happened after many frustrating nights while crying out to God. Her mantra during this season was "I am a child of obedience. I will not partner with a spirit of fantasy."

If you have had a pattern of self-talk in your life that came from partnering with a familiar spirit, the patterns in your life that supported its existence may still remain. It is possible that daily acts of obedience are required to take the "normal" self-talk voice captive. Severing ties with these familiar spirits can be difficult. For example, Dawna first felt her situation with this issue was unfair. Her thoughts ran as follows: *This is not fair, this is not fun, and this is not right. God,*

I don't like these guardrails. How come I can't just pick my own dreams? However, obeying the Holy Spirit led to her receiving God's dreams. After years of living with false comfort, Dawna began to hear Him speak and comfort her during difficult times.

Notice Dawna's courage in this simple yet painful act of obedience. Recognizing an ungodly partnership in her life, she focused on replacing it with God's presence. Some of us have similar issues so ingrained that we do not even know they exist. Through the eyes of friends and mentors, the Holy Spirit's promptings, and Scripture, we can find hindrances that hold us back and replace them with Kingdom principles.

Even if hindrances seem harmless, we must disarm them. Lies and strongholds from the enemy usually begin in slight, deceptive ways rather than with bold, frontal assaults. Over time, as we allow ourselves to partner with the enemy's schemes, their lies develop. As in Dawna's example above, it may take many times of standing firm against the enemy to keep the doors from which you have been delivered closed.

When we receive healing or breakthrough from the Lord, it is our job to walk it out. There is no specific amount of time set aside as a formula for standing against the places we have been delivered from. It simply comes down to "out-patience-ing" the enemy. Until you feel that shift occur, you must remain bold and steadfast. Walking in obedience to the Lord, you will overcome the enemy's schemes. Through submitting to His will, you will become a powerful warrior:

> *If My people who are called by My name humble themselves,*
> *and pray and seek My face and turn from their wicked ways,*
> *then I will hear from heaven and will forgive their sin and*
> *heal their land* (2 Chronicles 7:14).

Confess your sins to one another, and pray for one another so that you may be healed (James 5:16).

Children, obey your parents in the Lord, for this is right. "Honor your father and mother"—which is the first commandment with a promise—so that it may go well with you and that you may enjoy long life on the earth (Ephesians 6:1-3 NIV).

These verses show the benefits of obedience and accountability. It is important not to close ourselves off from the godly advice of our spouses, friends, parents, and mentors. Obviously, some people in our lives are not safe to submit to. Boundaries are helpful methods of resolution.

As children of obedience, we become powerful by listening to the counsel of those who are for us and by saying yes to God. Allowing others to speak into our life increases our field of vision. It gives us an extra set of eyes to view our life and situation through. This enables us to have a greater perspective when the enemy hurls opposition toward us. It is always beneficial to have people we can trust and submit to.

Wielding the weapon of obedience is key for those who desire to walk in pursuit of God. If you find yourself struggling to obey God, see if you partner with a lens that makes obedience seem controlling or harsh. You will never see the full manifestation of God unless you believe and see Him as He is—loving and good.

To renounce ties with control and a false lens, repeat this prayer:

Thank You, Lord, for revealing Your heart for me. Thank You that obedience does not mean I get to be controlled by You or anyone. It simply means You know what's best for me and desire to see my heart succeed. I hand this lens to You in Jesus's name. I receive the lens that You are good and have my best at heart. Amen.

As an act of prophetic demonstration, physically remove whichever spiritual glasses through which you are seeing life. Replace them with whichever lens God gives you. Allow yourself to see through His perspective. Like any loving father, the Lord does not want to control you. Instead, He wants to see you safe and restored.

| Group Discussion Questions |

1. Do you find it hard to allow people to speak into your life or challenge your decisions?

2. Do you get defensive when people question your motives?

3. Have you been harmed by anyone in authority over you?

| Activation |

1. Forgive anyone in your life who had authority over you who caused you harm.

2. Ask Jesus to show you where He was when this happened.

3. Ask Father God what lie this experience taught you.

4. Ask Him what truth He wants to reveal to you.

5. Ask the Holy Spirit to show any ungodly practices with which you have been partnering.

6. Ask Jesus to forgive you for partnering with them.

7. Renounce partnership with any lies.

8. Ask the Holy Spirit to give you strength daily to refuse agreement with this spirit or ungodly practice.

9. Begin walking daily in obedience to God by standing firm against the draw of this spirit.

10. Ponder this verse:

Therefore take up the whole armor of God, that you may be able to withstand in the evil day, and having done all, to stand firm (Ephesians 6:13).

| Suggested Materials |

De Silva, Dawna. *Wielding the Weapon of Obedience.* CD/DVD.

Silk, Danny. *Culture of Honor: Sustaining a Supernatural Environment.* Shippensburg, PA: Destiny Image, 2009 Print.

WHAT'S NEXT?

Attaining physical, spiritual, and emotional health takes time. Do not be discouraged if the enemy tries to ensnare you with old, familiar patterns. Instead, bring your needs before the Father, Son, and Holy Spirit.

If you wish to find out more about Sozo or are interested in scheduling a session, visit Bethel Sozo's website at www.bethelsozo.com. Beneath the "Sozo Network" and "Regional Directors" tabs, information about nearby Sozo team practitioners is available.

We hope you have enjoyed studying the keys to freedom found within this book. We expect, through faithful practice, you will begin to live powerfully and see the enemy's strongholds crumble. Jesus' promises of abundant life are yours to be encountered.

Remember, you are no longer a slave to sin. Because of Christ's sacrifice, you have been made heirs to God. Everything you need has already been paid for. He is expectantly waiting for you to seek Him out.

> It is the glory of God to conceal things, but the glory of kings
> is to search things out (Proverbs 25:2).

Blessings on your journey as you seek the things of God and apply them to your life.

Blessings,
DAWNA and TERESA

GLOSSARY

A

AGGRESSIVE BEHAVIOR: A domineering, forceful, or assaultive verbal or physical action intended to harm or influence another person.

APHESIS: A Greek word meaning "to be released from bondage" or "forgiveness of sins."

AUTHORITIES: Demonic powers that hold spiritual authority over regions, places, or persons.

B

BENI JOHNSON: Senior pastor at Bethel Church, author, and speaker. She has a call to impart joyful intercession and is passionate about health and wholeness.

BILL JOHNSON: Senior pastor of Bethel Church, author and speaker, known for his healing and miracle ministry. Bill teaches that we owe the world an encounter with God and a Gospel without power is not the Gospel Jesus preached.

BODY: A person's physical self.

BREAKTHROUGH: A sudden increase in knowledge, understanding, or healing.

BROADCASTS: Messages of hate, sin, slavery, immorality, or whatever else the enemy wants to impart over a person, place, or region.

BULLY MINDSET: A mindset where one believes he must protect himself by causing harm to others or causing them to fear.

C

SOZO CLIENT: Person who schedules a Sozo session.

COLORED LENSES: False lenses that tint the way one sees life; these lenses result from partnering with skewed perspectives—viewpoints developed in childhood, mostly incorrect, which we embrace to cope with life's mysteries.

CRAFTY SUGGESTIONS: Lies satan presents while disguised as an angel of light; seemingly innocent at first, but as one partners with them, a strong opposing spirit develops.

D

DELIVERANCE: The act of casting out or displacing demonic attachments from a person.

DIASŌZŌ: A Greek word with its roots extending from sōzō but carrying the meanings of "preserving through danger, to bring safely through, and to keep from perishing"; it also can be "to save, cure one who is sick, or bring him through."

DISCERNMENT: The quality of being able to comprehend the spiritual realm; the ability to perceive what God is doing.

E

ENEMY: Dark or negative force; satan.

EXCHANGE: When one gives Father God, Jesus, or the Holy Spirit a lie, a truth is given in return; so one can exchange a lie for a truth.

EXORCISE: To force an evil spirit to leave through the power of Holy Spirit.

EXORCIST: One who expels (an evil spirit) by commanding with power from Holy Spirit.

F

FALSE TRUTH: An ungodly reasoning that poses as a righteous belief that integrates into our belief systems and disrupts the flow of healthy living.

FATHER GOD: Creator; the first Person of the Godhead.

FATHER LADDER: A main tool the Sozo Ministry uses to help clarify the connections between lies that have been learned from childhood and the relationships we have formed with each member of the Godhead.

FEAR DOOR: The first and most frequently encountered of the Four Doors. Inside this door is found worry, unbelief, the need for control, anxiety, isolation, apathy, and drug and alcohol addictions.

FORGIVENESS: The act of being forgiven or forgiving; No longer blaming someone for pain and suffering; no longer requiring payment of a debt.

FOUR DOORS: A main tool the Sozo Ministry uses to identify strongholds in a person's life.

FRANCIS FRANGIPANE: A Christian evangelical minister and author of *The Three Battlegrounds: An In-Depth View of the Three Arenas of Spiritual Warfare: The Mind, the Church and the Heavenly Places.*

H

HATRED/BITTERNESS DOOR: The second of the Four Doors. Inside this door is bitterness, envy, gossip, slander, anger, and self-hatred (low self-worth).

HERO MINDSET: A mindset where one believes that no matter what, he or she is powerful and has no need to be a threat or be threatened.

HINDRANCE: A negative mindset or demonic attachment that makes the act of connecting with God difficult.

HOLY SPIRIT: God's Spirit; the third Person of the Godhead.

I

IAOMAI: A Greek word meaning "to cure, heal, to make whole (free from error and sins, to bring one's salvation)."

IDENTIFICATION: The act of discovering which lies a person believes.

INTERCESSION: The act of interceding; prayer, petition, or entreaty in favor of another.

J

JESUS: God's Son; the second Person of the Godhead.

JEHOVAH-TSIDKENU: A Greek name for Jesus, meaning "the Lord our righteousness."

K

KINGDOM: Eternity worldview; Heaven on earth; God's dominion on earth as it is in Heaven.

L

LIE: An untrue or inaccurate statement that misleads or deceives.

M

MAMMON: Wealth personified; money deified; greed and avarice; spirit of Mammon.

MEDIATOR: One who mediates, who occupies in a middle position.

O

OCCULT DOOR: The fourth and final of the Four Doors. Inside this door is astrology, fortune-telling, tarot cards, séances, Ouija boards, manipulation, participation in covens, casting curses, and witchcraft practices.

ORPHAN SPIRIT: The mindset of powerlessness that works to undermine Christ's adoptive spirit.

P

PABLO BOTTARI: Author and internationally recognized authority on the ministry of deliverance; he created the "Ten Steps" tool for deliverance ministry.

PHEUGŌ: A Greek word meaning "fleeing away/saved by flight."

PRESENTING JESUS: A tool used to find where lies originated in a person's life.

POVERTY SPIRIT: The mindset of lack; attitude of inferiority; spirit of poverty.

POWERS: See AUTHORITIES.

R

RENUNCIATION: The act of renouncing a harmful or destructive mindset.

ROOT: Where a lie begins.

RULERS: See AUTHORITIES.

S

SEXUAL SIN DOOR: The third of the Four Doors. Inside this door is adultery, pornography, fornication, lewdness, molestation, fantasy, rape, and entertaining lustful thoughts.

SHIFTING ATMOSPHERES: The practice of identifying what is being broadcast over a region, place, or person and displacing or turning off these broadcasts.

SŌTĒRIA: A Greek word meaning "saved," which indicates deliverance and salvation.

SŌZŌ: The Greek word translated "saved, healed, and delivered."

SOZO MINISTER: A person who facilitates a Sozo, listening to Father God, Jesus, and Holy Spirit while guiding the client through inner healing.

SOZO MINISTRY: An inner healing and deliverance ministry aimed at discovering the root hindrances blocking one's personal connection with the Father, Son, and Holy Spirit.

SOZO SESSION: A time for a Sozo minister to sit down with a client; to partner with Father God, Jesus, and the Holy Spirit to experience wholeness.

SOUL: A person's mind, will, and emotions.

SPIRIT: The force within a person that is believed to give the body life, energy, and power.

SPIRIT OF ADOPTION: The Father's spiritual adoption of His sons and daughters; what we receive when we enter the Kingdom through accepting Jesus's sacrifice for us on the cross.

STEPHEN DE SILVA: Co-founder of De Silva Ministries; author, speaker, and founder of Prosperous Soul Ministries.

STRONGHOLD: A deeply ingrained and habitual obstacle and hindrance that holds one back from one's destiny.

T

TEN STEPS: Pablo Bottari's effective inner healing and deliverance tool; a basis for the Four Doors.

THERAPEUŌ: A Greek word meaning "to serve, do service and to heal, cure, and restore to health."

TRANSFORMATION CENTER: The main campus for the Sozo and Shabar Ministry in Redding, California.

U

UNFORGIVENESS: The inability or unwillingness to forgive.

V

VICTIM MINDSET: A mindset where one believes everyone is after him, that he is powerless to life's circumstances.

VICTORIOUS MINDSET: A mindset that empowers people to make choices and live powerfully; Christ's mindset.

VILLAIN MINDSET: A mindset where one believes he is better than those who hurt him so he must protect himself by causing others to fear him.

All definitions of Greek words from *Strong's Concordance*

ABOUT THE AUTHORS

Dawna De Silva is the founder and co-leader with Teresa Liebscher of the International Bethel Sozo Ministry. She and her husband, Stephen De Silva, have ministered from Bethel for the past twenty years as well as preaching, speaking, and authoring books. Dawna's manual on Shifting Atmospheres has become a sought-after tool for daily empowerment. Whether training Sozo, preaching, shifting atmospheres, or ministering prophetically, Dawna releases people, churches, and cities into new vision and freedom. No matter how traumatic the wounding, Dawna ministers with authority and gentleness, imparting hope and healing.

Teresa Liebscher is a co-leader of the Bethel Sozo ministry headquartered at Bethel Church in Redding, CA. She is also the founder and leader of the Shabar ministry. The Bethel Sozo ministry was birthed in 1997 and the Shabar ministry in 2006. Teresa travels the world training, mentoring and ministering in both Bethel Sozo and Shabar ministry. Her passion in all areas of her ministering life is to not only connect individuals with each member of the Godhead, but also to make sure that connection is healthy.

OTHER BOOKS BY
DAWNA DE SILVA AND TERESA LIEBSCHER

Atmospheres 101 by Dawna De Silva

Life After Integration by Teresa Liebscher